STRUCTURING THE PAST

THE USE OF COMPUTERS IN HISTORY

by

JANICE L. REIFF

PUBLISHED BY THE AMERICAN HISTORICAL ASSOCIATION

Structuring the Past:

The Use of Computers in History

WITHDRAWN

by

Janice L. Reiff

PUBLISHED BY THE AMERICAN HISTORICAL ASSOCIATION

JANICE L. REIFF is Jesse Hauk Shera Assistant Professor of History at Case Western Reserve University in Cleveland, Ohio. Dr. Reiff has been actively involved in encouraging the use of computers by historians for many years, notably at the Newberry Library in its Institutes in Quantitative Methods in History. Janice Reiff also serves as contributing editor for computer applications to *Perspectives*, the American Historical Association's newsletter.

AHA Pamphlets Editor: Roxanne Myers Spencer

© 1991 by the American Historical Association

Supported by funding from the Exxon Education Foundation

Illustrations courtesy of the John M. Wing Foundation,
The Newberry Library, Chicago.

ISBN: 0-87229-050-6
Library of Congress catalog card number: 91-075431
Printed in the United States of America

DCP . 750M 4/94

CONTENTS

Preface

§

*T*he origins of this pamphlet lay in a conference sponsored by the American Historical Association's Committee on Quantitative Research in History, with support from the Exxon Education Foundation. The conference, "Quantification, Computers, and Teaching History," was held in November 1984 at Amherst College. Historians from across the country discussed the possibilities and limitations of the use of quantitative techniques for teaching history. The exchange was, as might be expected, lively. Debates over what historical phenomena could and could not be quantified shaped certain sessions. The issue of minimal standards for statistical competency informed others. Throughout the conference, the topic of computing kept reappearing.

Reflecting, perhaps, the state of computing in the mid-1980s, there was no real consensus about the role of the computer. Many of the "quantifiers" took it for granted that computers were already—and would continue to be—important tools of their methodology. At the same time, they insisted that it would be a mistake to give computers and computer applications any kind of intellectual status, because to do so would be like elevating the typewriter. Other participants demonstrated how they were beginning to use *microcomputers* for teaching. Only a very few of those in attendance were willing to argue that computers might have an impact on research and teaching that could only be guessed at then, and even fewer were willing to believe them.

This pamphlet serves as a kind of vindication for the position of those early "prophets." When a decision had to be made about what to do with the remaining unexpended funds from that conference, both the American Historical Association and the Exxon Education Foundation felt a pamphlet on the use of computers in teaching and researching history would be an appropriate use of the money. The years between the conference and that decision showed how dramatic changes in computing had been; therefore, it seemed likely that historians would want to learn more about the possibilities for computers within the profession. The years between the decision to do the pamphlet and its appearance only confirms the wisdom of that initial decision.

What follows is an attempt to describe the current state of computer *hardware* and *software* with two primary goals in mind: (1) to stimulate those who read the pamphlet to take advantage of the possibilities associated with the computer, and (2) to encourage historians to participate more directly in the discussions about how these information technologies will be used in the colleges, universities, libraries, museums, and archives that are so important to our professional lives.[1] In addition, the pamphlet has to meet another goal as well—to serve as a kind of reference guide for those who have basic questions about computing.

To meet those goals, this volume will not follow the familiar format of most computer-related handbooks with a chapter on *word processing,* another on *spreadsheets,* another on *databases,* and so on. That particular structure reveals much about the current state of microcomputing, but it does little to break us away from those now common categories of applications. Most of us as computer consumers have neither the knowledge nor the need to push the boundaries of those categories. Because we can type our manuscripts in Microsoft Word or Word Perfect, we are happy to keep buying the *upgrades* to the programs that contain all the latest bells and whistles in word processing, but we pay little if any attention to changes in *desktop publishing* or *information retrieval* systems. Yet, as historians we consistently raise the question of the appropriateness of categories. If Robert Darnton's "French inspector sorts his files" differently to provide new insights into eighteenth-century French society, then as historians we should try to re-sort those computer categories to make them more useful tools for our own research.[2]

This pamphlet attempts to do that by using a different organizational structure. The opening chapter is a challenge to consider ways in which computers might eventually impact our work and our discipline. Subsequent chapters are structured around the way historians approach their craft. These consider the specific tasks we regularly undertake and suggest ways in which we might use computers to facilitate them. Those chapters also will include a discussion of the possible implications of computer usage, examples of how they are currently being used in history and related disciplines, and a bibliography for those interested in pursuing the topic further.

Ideally, this organization will serve the first two purposes for the pamphlet. To serve the third purpose, that of being a basic reference guide, the pamphlet will rely on another organizational technique that combines traditional footnotes with the logic of the *hypertext* programs that are attracting a great deal of attention for both text manipulation and teaching. Anytime a word in the text is italicized (like hypertext above), an entry appears in the glossary. Similarly, if a software package, organization, or other resource appears in the Helvetica *type font*, the Resource Guide in Appendix B contains more detailed information on it. Although flipping pages is perhaps more difficult than pointing and *clicking* on a computer screen as one would do in a hypertext file, it is a technique with which we are all familiar from decades of reading books. These guides should serve to translate the computer jargon to readers and to provide suggestions for where to find more information as needed.

A final caveat is in order here. This pamphlet cannot be a *"state-of-the-art"* effort. Improvements in computer hardware and software occur almost daily; the pamphlet will be out of date before it is ever bound. Individuals working on brilliant teaching applications will complete their efforts soon after this appears. In that sense, a collection such as this can be of only limited value. If, however, the pamphlet suggests opportunities for facilitating our research or teaching, or makes historians more knowledgeable participants in campus discussions about the role of computers and *telecommunications* in the curriculum or the library, then it has achieved its goal of helping us make these technologies our own.

Nor can this pamphlet even attempt to survey or evaluate the wide range of hardware and software currently available or the *vaporware* that has yet to appear. There is simply too much out there to provide any systematic or fair analysis. Fortunately, there are guides like *Software Digest* that serve as a computer user's *Consumer Reports,* and computer magazines that regularly review different products. In addition, the observation one contributor so wisely made about word processors—that the choice of a word processor is somewhat like the choice of a favorite color—actually extends to other kinds of software as well. Many people can make a piece of software they know well do things that might actually be much simpler with a different piece of software. Yet, for them, their way is the best solution because they don't need to buy new software or invest time in learning it. The fact that a piece of software appears by name in this volume should not be seen as an endorsement. Instead, it is included because it serves as an appropriate example of a piece of software that a historian has used to accomplish a particular task.

This pamphlet could not have been completed without the assistance of several organizations and individuals. The Exxon Foundation graciously allowed the American Historical Association to use unexpended funds from a previous award for the conference,"Quantification, Computers, and Teaching History," for the production of this pamphlet. James B. Gardner had the original idea for both the pamphlet and the author. Maris Deneke worked long hours in the libraries at Case Western Reserve University and Cleveland State University uncovering relevant materials, learning much about computers in the process. Academic Computing and Network Services at Northwestern University made its library of computer materials and journals available to me, and the Newberry Library and the Regenstein Library at the University of Chicago provided many supplemental materials. The staff at the Newberry Library, especially John Aubrey, patiently walked me through *OCLC*, VTLS, and the world of library automation. The Chicago Metro History Fair made its *laser printer* and *scanner* available to create the manuscript. Paul Gehl, curator of the Wing Collection at the Newberry Library, took time to introduce me to the world of sixteenth- and seventeenth-century books and printing technology as he helped locate appropriate illustrations. Ken Cain photographed all the illustrations. The *Social Science Computer Review*, edited by G. David Garson, was the best single reference for uncovering the state of computing in many related disciplines. Jim Barrett, Mike Grossberg, Nancy Fitch, Carl Ubbelohde, Terry Reiff, and Laura Edwards read parts or all of the manuscript and offered many valuable suggestions. Of course, the mistakes that remain in the document are mine and not theirs. Roxanne Myers Spencer, the American Historical Association's pamphlets editor, did the final editing, design, layout, and production.

Thanks are also due the many people who sent materials in response to the notice in *Perspectives*, the American Historical Association's newsletter. Some of their individual contributions are noted in the text itself. The efforts of these individuals are also those that have led the way toward incorporating computers into the world of historical teaching and research, shaping the technology to their own ends. The debt to them is substantial.

Finally, for those who might be interested, this original document was composed on a Toshiba 1200HD and an IBM AT using Microsoft Word, version 5. Notes were taken and information stored in the database program AskSam. Images were scanned using Hewlett-Packard's ScanJet scanner and Scangal software. The initial manuscript was produced with Word on an HP LaserJet II printer. Text was imported into Nota Bene for text editing, then, for page design and layout, into Ventura Desktop Publisher, version 2.0 on an Epson Equity II+ and an IBM PS/2. Camera-ready copy was printed on a NEC Silentwriter2 290.

I

$\mathcal{S}$TRUCTURING THE $\mathcal{P}$AST

§

*I*n his challenging book, *Turing's Man*, Douglas Bolter argues that the computer is a "defining technology."[1] Like the mechanical clock and the steam engine before it, the computer has caused us to revise how we think about fundamental aspects of our lives and our world. Published in 1984, the book reveals several ways in which computers have already changed how American society thinks about and implements a variety of activities. Bolter also predicts that the changes yet to come will be even more monumental. He does not argue that the results of this computer revolution all have been beneficial; indeed, he suggests a side as dark as that of the Industrial Revolution. Nor does he contend that all of the lavish claims made about the computer will ever be met. Many will be dead-end; some might be impossible. Yet, he argues, and most would have to agree, that the computer and its applications have already transformed many aspects of our lives.

If Bolter is correct, we as historians have to address a series of critical questions about the impact of computers and related technologies on our professional lives. What has been the role of computers in writing history? Have computers changed the way we ply our craft? Have computers opened up new avenues for structuring and probing historical evidence? If so, might these new modes of inquiry alter the way we define specific fields within history and other disciplines? Finally, do long-term developments in computer technologies even offer the possibility of redefining the hierarchies within the historical profession?

Few would argue that computers have had a major impact on how many of us do our work. Historians are as likely to write with a word processor on a *microcomputer* as with a typewriter. We regularly organize our notes on computers. *Modems* inside those same microcomputers let us access library *on-line* catalogs at our home institutions and at other libraries that provide *dial-up* facilities. For those willing to pay for such resources, bibliographic *database* services make indexes, abstracts, and even full texts available by modem. The rest of us have to content ourselves with going to a library and using *CD-ROM* versions of the same services that were recently only available in printed form. *BITNET* and *Internet* facilitate rapid communication throughout much of the world.

Prospective authors and publishers share information on *software* and *disk compatibility.* Database programs let us store and retrieve our own bibliographies. The list of such examples could be continued indefinitely.

MAKING A 'DEFINING' CHANGE

Computers have clearly invaded the world of the historian. Each development has made certain of our tasks potentially faster, more convenient, and less repetitious. Yet, it is fair to ask whether any of these developments have really changed the way in which we "do history." Has the computer been a defining technology for our discipline? Right now, the answer to that question is, "Not yet." Surveys of the use of computers in the historical profession continue to find relatively little use beyond *word processing,* especially when compared to other disciplines in the humanities and social sciences. However, we may stand at a threshold of change. Whether it comes into being depends largely on ongoing improvements in related technologies such as image and text *scanning* and *data communications,* continued declining costs for storage and speed, and, most problematic, a commitment on someone's part to the preservation of historical sources in *machine-readable* form. It also depends on the willingness of historians to use the technology in new and creative ways. Let me suggest briefly three areas in which these kinds of changes might take place.

One critical area where the computer could make a "defining" change is in the use of historical evidence. Evidence, and the interpretations based on it, are of fundamental concern to the entire historical process. The nature of that evidence and how it is interpreted has always provoked considerable debate. Types of evidence help to define subfields within history. Intellectual historians emphasize one kind of evidence, diplomatic historians another, social historians still another.

Although much identification of types of evidence with certain subdisciplines results from the data's appropriateness for answering particular questions, there is also an issue of priorities involved. Historians do not exclude evidence that they consider important. They do, however, decide that some sources are marginal to their work, given the amount of effort required to use them. For example, a person studying ideas about philanthropy in late nineteenth-century America might not consider looking at the payrolls of the philanthropists' firms to see how their corporate and business actions corresponded to their public postures and gifts. Nor would someone who has spent years collecting payroll, census, and corporate information necessarily read every foreign-language labor newspaper for mention of the company or community unless there was reason to think doing so would dramatically affect one's own conclusions. The time required to organize years of payrolls for thousands of workers or to read years of nineteenth-century German, Italian, Swedish, Norwegian, and Polish newspapers promises only marginal returns.

What if, however, these sources were available in machine-readable form as well as on microfilm? The technology now exists that converts microfilm images to machine-readable form. Combined with sophisticated database software, the time/return balance that is so important to all of us could change dramatically. One could *search* previously unindexed documents quickly for any word or combination of words and immediately retrieve the text. Hours of unrelated research would become minutes of very focused searching. Even more time would be saved if these texts, previously available only in different archives all over the country, could be made available either on-line or on CD-ROM for use at home or in the office. Suddenly, not only would the researcher be able to describe how Swedes and Germans occupied different jobs and earned different wages but also how the two groups perceived that differential treatment. Similarly, without much more time or effort, the payrolls could be perused individually or summarized according to categories to provide a much richer insight into the workings of the company and, perhaps, to the philanthropist's own corporate practices.

If these examples were expanded to include different sources from different countries and different time periods, would the discipline of history remain unchanged? For example, comparative history might flourish if computers eased the research constraints on time, distance, and individual expense.[2] Would even more comparative analysis be encouraged if the computer could provide a reliable translation of a foreign language document, a possibility that is coming closer and closer to reality? Might some of the heated debates over the nature of history, the validity of particular historical actors and issues, and the appropriateness and applicability of different sources moderate in the face of easy access to the other side's evidence?

Methodology, or the way in which we move from evidence to interpretation, is a second critical area where qualitative change might occur. The importance of this issue struck me dramatically very early one morning in the Jordan River Valley. As my guide described the walls and cultural areas that he saw, I nodded appreciatively, yet saw only a hill of indistinguishable clay and rock. More daunting was the realization that my task was to use a computer to organize the stones, potsherds, and bones visible so that he could reconstruct the social and cultural system that the excavators were hoping to find.

In fact, varieties of computer programs exist that help to do just that, not only in archaeology but in literature, sociology, economics, political science, musicology, and art. Large-scale initiatives are underway to arrive at standards for data organization that will allow the greatest possible flexibility in handling evidence. These efforts, if successful, will mean that texts, images, numeric data, musical notation, and other disparate forms of information can be stored in a *format* compatible with an ever-expanding number of programs that can be used to analyze them. This will open opportunities for exploring data in ways that have, in the past, been limited to those either with vast budgets or very specialized training and skills.

For example, the computer has made spatial analysis of all kinds infinitely easier. Mapping, both physical and conceptual, can be done using software programs that have become increasingly more powerful and *user-friendly*. Might these programs, combined with more available evidence, encourage more historians to use techniques that have only been the domain of geographers? Would the availability of software that analyzes the structure and content of text enhance the efforts of historians involved in the debates over language and its importance in understanding the past? If it were easy to do, might those who challenge this approach try it, using their own data in conjunction with their own methods, to see if they are complementary? Quantitative analysis might no longer seem as daunting or inappropriate if it were accessible to more people. One could even experiment with more sophisticated mathematical models to explore historical evidence. Surely we have all considered at least once that chaos theory might be the single most convincing explanation of certain aspects of the past.[3] Given the right software, one could construct a model to do just that.

LONG-TERM IMPLICATIONS

What are the long-term implications of these software and *hardware* developments? First, they will make more methodological approaches available to more people. This does not mean that everyone will become expert in linguistic analysis because of a software program stored on *personal computers* or on a campus *network*. Nor will someone necessarily understand the mathematical complexities of event analysis just by working with the appropriate software. It does mean, however, that one could experiment with the approach to see if it reveals anything useful about a specific piece of research. If it does, then the methodology might be pursued either through developing an expertise or by consulting an expert. Even if it does not, the process of thinking about one's own evidence from another methodological perspective can only broaden the final interpretive result.

Potentially, these new computer possibilities stand to blur disciplinary lines even more. If what distinguishes disciplines are methodology, questions, and data, then the lines between the various social sciences and humanities will become less clear as approaches and data become transferable, not just to a few disciplines, as is now the case, but to many. This may be particularly true for historians because, if historical evidence becomes as accessible as suggested above, then one of the characteristics that most distinguishes our profession, that is, that we study the past, might become more common to other disciplines as well. If so, the debates over the valid questions of history might take on whole new levels of complexity.

The third area where computers might effect a defining change may well be in the hierarchy of the profession. A caveat is necessary here. There will always be brilliant historians as compared to the rest of us, just as there will always be a hierarchy of "better" universities and colleges with more money to spend on resources for research and teaching. There has often been a strong relationship between the two, often with the resources of the latter encouraging the evaluation of the former. Faculty members at institutions with fewer resources for travel funds, libraries, and release time have found it more difficult to publish, the standard by which much of the academic world measures. If all the books and archives found in all the great research institutions were available to anyone with a computer, wouldn't it be easier for those who are not at major research institutions to compete with those who are? And, if so, might not other concerns like the quality of life or the environment become more important criteria for defining institutional hierarchies for both students and faculty?

The potential exists for computers to become a defining technology for the historical profession. What we as historians should realize, perhaps more than most, is that those who can use such technologies in a creative way can gain most from them. Those who try to stand in the way of or who ignore such technologies have, traditionally, suffered because of those actions. Perhaps, as a profession, we can successfully learn such lessons from the past.

II

COLLECTING INFORMATION

§

*P*erhaps no single task consumes as much of a historian's time and energy as collecting information. We devote countless hours to reading journals to keep abreast of the newest research in our fields. We scan book reviews and footnotes to decide which books we have to read and which books we browse through. Years spent in libraries have taught us to master card catalogs and indexes. By trial and error we have mastered the unique organizational logic of various archives. We skim the tables of contents and indexes of some books for facts and read others carefully to understand the arguments and interpretations. Studying maps gives us the geographic orientation we need; photographs, drawings, and portraits provide visual images. We hear papers and attend seminars to learn from the insights of our peers. In every instance, we are collecting information.

Computers excel at manipulating information very quickly, so it is not surprising that their impact on this aspect of historical endeavor has been substantial. Most major libraries now have *on-line* catalogs. Archivists discuss the *MARC format* for their collections. Dissertation abstracts are available on *CD-ROM*, as are most of the major scholarly indexes. For a fee, a home computer owner with a *modem* can use the services of such companies as Dialog to *search* thousands of bibliographic *databases*.

This profusion of computerized information is not limited to contemporary or post-1970 information. Oxford University Press markets an electronic edition of the complete works of Shakespeare on either 5¼" or 3½" *disks*. The entire body of ancient Greek texts, the *Thesaurus Linguae Graecae*, has been available on its own *workstation* since the 1970s. The Perseus Project at Harvard is expanding the computerized Greek world even further, incorporating not only the texts in Greek and English, but a dictionary, an atlas, site plans, some five thousand to ten thousand images, encyclopedia entries, and general and specialized articles appropriate to the topic. Rutgers University continues to develop a medieval database; the University of Chicago's American and French Research on the Treasury of the French Language (ARTFL) project provides *dial-up access* to all the French literary texts of the nineteenth century. Data from a wide variety of sources are available in *machine-readable* form from the Inter-University Consortium for Social and Political Research.

Laptop and *notebook computers* have begun to change how we organize our own research notes. From the Archives Nationales to the Schlesinger Library, individual scholars have abandoned note cards and begun to enter notes, citations, and bibliographic information directly into the computer. Scholars have created their own machine-readable archives, which are changing the way we think about even our own research.

At first glance, the range of existing and potential applications is so fluid and vast that it seems to defy understanding. There are common threads, however, between the different kinds of programs—those organized using databases, *hypermedia*, and *spreadsheets*, for example—that when considered together help to explain present uses and suggest future ones.

LIBRARY ON-LINE CATALOGS

Perhaps the easiest place to begin this discussion of different ways of managing historical information with computers is with databases, because historians come into contact with them more often than any other kind of computer application except *word processing*. To understand databases, the most intuitive entry point is in libraries and their on-line catalogs. Libraries serve as an appropriate portal into this rapidly expanding area for two reasons. First, so much historical research begins in a library that most of us have developed at least a minimal familiarity with how a library database works, whether it be VTLS, NOTIS, or some other system. Second, the logic of these on-line systems serves as an excellent introduction to broader issues of information management that are important to understand if one is to take full advantage of existing *software* packages and databases.

At the heart of the on-line library catalog is a system not very different from the card catalog. With the card catalog, the researcher would search for a book using one of three approaches: look up the book's author(s), title, or subject matter. To find a book like E. P. Thompson's *Making of the English Working Class*, the user could look for the author entry (Thompson, Edward P.), the title entry (*Making of the English Working Class*), the subject entry (labor and laboring classes — Great Britain), or, using the shelf-list catalog, the call number. One book required at least four separate cards to allow researchers to find it from four different *paths*.

In an on-line system, each book is entered once. Instead of multiple entries, the computer software allows multiple access to the entry for one book. For example, entries on an on-line system (here VTLS) might appear on the *terminal* screen as:

CALL NUMBER:	HD8039.P152 U53 1987
AUTHOR:	Barrett, James R., 1950–
TITLE:	Work and community in the jungle: Chicago's packinghouse workers, 1894-1922 / James R. Barrett.
PUBLICATION:	Urbana: University of Illinois Press, c1987.
COLLATION:	xvi, 290 p., [7] leaves of plates: ill., ports.; 24 cm.
SERIES:	Working Class in American History
NOTE:	Includes bibliography and index.
SUBJECT:	Packinghouse workers — Illinois — Chicago — History
SUBJECT:	Community organization — Illinois — Chicago — History
SUBJECT:	Quality of work life — Illinois — Chicago — History
SUBJECT:	Mass production — Illinois — Chicago — History
SUBJECT:	Trade unions — Packinghouse workers — Illinois — Chicago — History

or

CALL NUMBER:	HD8079.C4 H57 1990
AUTHOR:	Hirsch, Eric L., 1952–
TITLE:	Urban Revolt: ethnic politics in the nineteenth-century. Chicago labor movement / Eric L. Hirsch.
PUBLICATION:	Berkeley: University of California Press, c1990.
COLLATION:	xvii, 253 p.: ill.; 24 cm.
NOTE:	Includes index.
NOTE:	Bibliography. p. 221–235.
SUBJECT:	Working class — Illinois — Chicago — History — 19th century.
SUBJECT:	Labor movement — Illinois — Chicago — History — 19th century.

To search for the Hirsch book by author, title, or subject, you could simply type A/HIRSCH, ERIC L.; T/URBAN REVOLT; OR S/WORKING CLASS — ILLINOIS — CHICAGO — HISTORY — 19TH CENTURY; where A/ indicates that you want an author search, T/ a title search, and S/ a subject search. Intuitively, this is exactly the same logic as using the card catalog. However, it also serves as an example of how databases work. Every database is composed of *records;* in the on-line catalog, each book represents one record. Each record is composed of *fields.* In the examples above, the field names are AUTHOR, TITLE, SUBJECT, and so on. The information assigned to those fields is what is searched when the computer is told by the A/, T/, or S/ to search in a particular field.

Just as the card catalog was organized alphabetically to facilitate finding a book, the on-line database is *indexed* or sorted in ways that help the computer find the record you want more quickly. Every on-line system has multiple indexes: one that is alphabetical by author, another alphabetical by title, another alphabetical by subject, and still another in numerical order by call number. When you indicate that you want to do an author search, the on-line system automatically uses the appropriate index to the database for that search. A search command of A/HIRSCH, ERIC L. will cause the database system to point immediately to any records that have Eric L. Hirsch as author, and these will appear on the terminal screen. A command of A/HIRSCH will find the first record (alphabetically in the index) that has an author with the last name Hirsch and then list entries for all authors with that name.

This type of *fixed-field database* searching, using exact information to locate the same information in fixed, preassigned fields, is quite efficient for the computer, which simply has to match a *string* of characters provided by the person using the on-line catalog with the string of characters stored in the initial positions of the corresponding field in the database. It does not, however, work as well for the person approaching the on-line library system with less specific knowledge.

For someone sitting in front of the computer terminal wanting to find books on the Chicago working class in the late-nineteenth and early-twentieth centuries, the task of finding appropriate texts is somewhat more awkward, as the subject listings for the two books noted above show. Even with a copy of the Library of Congress (LC) subject headings on hand, finding all the relevant volumes would be difficult. For example, entering S/WORKING CLASS — ILLINOIS — CHICAGO would find the Hirsch book but miss the Barrett book because the LC classification does not identify it there. In some systems, entering S/CHICAGO would find neither because the word Chicago is not the initial entry in the subject field.

To compensate for this dilemma, some on-line library systems have added *key word* searching capabilities. Instead of matching the initial characters of a predefined field, a word search looks for a particular word anywhere in the record for all the books in the database. Such a search is not efficient in computer terms. VTLS, for example, warns the user doing a word search that it could take a long time. Yet, the command W/CHICAGO would find both books, along with several thousand others. Some limits can be placed on that search to cut the number of books that meet the criterion. One is to tell the system to search for the word in a particular field. For example, W/T:CHICAGO would look for the word Chicago only in the title field. That speeds the search for the computer because it has only to look for the word in one field in the book record instead of the whole record. It would also locate only the books with the word Chicago in the title.

The other is to do a search on multiple key words *linked* by AND, OR, or NOT. For example, one could tell the computer to look for CHICAGO AND WORKERS (finding records that contain both the words Chicago and workers) or WORKERS OR WORKING CLASS (finding records that contain either the word workers or the words working class). In some systems, these so-called *Boolean* searches can be defined in one search; in others, searching for records that contain multiple words would require multiple searches that are subsequently joined. For example, to look for books that have the key words CHICAGO and either WORKERS or WORKING CLASS would involve four searches. The first, W/S:CHICAGO, would find all the books that have the key word Chicago in its subject list; the second, W/S:WORKERS, would find all the books with the word workers; and the third, W/S:WORKING CLASS would find those with the words working class. In each instance, the system would indicate how many books were found that met the criteria. The final search would read 1 AND (2 OR 3), that is, Chicago AND (workers OR working class). These would be the books of particular interest. In the most flexible on-line systems, steps two and three could be combined by entering the command W/S:WORK*, where the asterisk indicates that any word beginning with the four characters W,O,R,K should be included. Such *wild card* searches must be used with caution, however, because they sometimes result in so many matches that subsequent combinations cannot be made by the *host computer* system.

One final approach to the library on-line catalogs that can be of real value to historians is to browse through the catalog by call number. For those who found many valuable books by walking through the stacks, this provides the closest approximation to that experience while using a computer terminal. Having determined the Barrett book's call number, a person could find other books with the same call number by searching for call number HD8039.

The advantages of these various approaches to the library catalog suggest some of the ways that the computerization of information both speeds access to that information and permits greater flexibility in approaches to it. Information is also available at sites removed from the physical card catalog, even to home users, if the computerized library catalog has dial-up access. This represents another significant advantage, especially if the system includes circulation status. However, the limitations of such systems are equally obvious when comparing the difference between looking at the book entry on the screen and taking a book from the shelf and browsing through its table of contents, index, bibliography, maps, or photographs. Current on-line library catalogs cannot provide that further step because each record contains only the basic bibliographic information for the book.

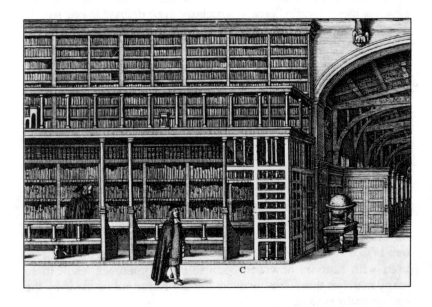

BIBLIOGRAPHIC DATABASES

Another kind of on-line database composed of information familiar to historians demonstrates the additional possibilities associated with database applications when more information is included in them. Dial-up services like Dialog and CD-ROM–based systems expand the options for retrieving information in large part because they expand the quantity and kind of information included in the databases. Dialog, for example, contains in excess of four hundred different bibliographic, numeric, and full-text databases. These databases span a wide range of topics and academic indexes from *Books in Print, Book Review Index, Dissertation Abstracts Online, Arts and Humanities Search (Arts and Humanities Citation Index), Humanities Index, America: History and Life, Social Science Index,* the *National Newspaper Index, Sociological Abstracts,* and *Economic Abstracts.*

Searching these databases on-line is similar to searching a library card catalog. Almost all have title, author, serial, journal, key word, and Boolean searches, as well as other types particular to the database. What differentiates them most from the library catalog searches is the amount of information available to search. To locate dissertations or master's theses on Chicago workers in *Dissertation Abstracts Online,* the searcher would have access not only to author, title, and subject fields but also to the abstract of the thesis supplied by the author. Moreover, because of *KWIC (keyword in context)* searching capabilities, the searcher can be more specific about the relationship between the words being searched. If wanted, the search can look for the combination of words only if they appear within the same paragraph, the same sentence, or next to each other. Once a dissertation is selected, the text of the abstract appears on the screen, providing the searcher with far more information than was available in the subject listings on the library on-line catalog.

Other on-line databases and services offer other types of information. CARL (the Colorado Alliance of Research Libraries), for example, has created an on-line system that gives users access to the tables of contents of all the journals in the libraries in their cooperative system. Begun in 1988, by July of 1990 there were already citations for more than one million articles available, using Uncover, the search programs specially developed for CARL. The system is available to other academic institutions and has an option that allows users to search and then request the full text of some articles, either on-line or via *fax* at a minimal charge. Plans are now underway between H. W. Wilson and University Microfilms International to develop and market a social science image database to be available on-line that will provide the complete text and all the graphic images (tables, charts, photographs) from journals that appear in *Social Science Index*. This system will also include a mechanism for letting searchers get copies of the articles located.

Although the discussion above focuses on printed materials, similar developments are proceeding, if at a somewhat slower rate, in making archival and museum materials available and accessible using the computer. Archivists throughout the United States have developed a standard format for on-line classification of archival holdings (MARC) and are beginning to share this information through the *OCLC* and *RLIN networks*. The same process is also taking place throughout the world, although somewhat different standards are emerging abroad. These developments in archival computerization are closely watched because, just as access is now possible to some European libraries via telephone lines, hopes exist that researchers will eventually have on-line access to collection information anywhere in the world.

EXISTING DATABASE APPLICATIONS

Considering a small-scale database in detail might provide some insight into the possibilities associated with computerized databases as they become increasingly more comprehensive and inclusive. One such database currently under development is the Perseus Project at Harvard University. By the end of 1993, the Perseus database will contain between fifty and one hundred *megabytes* of textual data and from five thousand to ten thousand images. Included in it will be the full text of the major Greek authors (in both Greek and English); basic research tools such as a dictionary, an atlas, site plans, and encyclopedia entries; relevant articles for both the generalist and the specialist; video narratives; and a book-length overview of Greek civilization. The project leader describes the database as:

> "For the student, Perseus will provide a small library. For the scholar, this environment will contain a number of tools that are not otherwise available and, in some cases, would not be possible outside of the electronic medium."[1]

This particular database is organized using hypermedia, a form of information management system rapidly growing in popularity, that incorporates most of the data classification and *retrieval* possibilities discussed above, but offers the added dimension of linking words and fields within records into other records that are logically connected in some way. Following are some examples of what options are available to users of Perseus. A student watching one of the short video presentations on the Temple of Apollo at Delphi could pause the video to find out more about Delphi by requesting more specific information. If a map would be useful, the student could call up a map of Greece, indicating the location of the city or *zooming* first to a topographic map of the region around Delphi and then to site plans for the temple itself. If a brief encyclopedia-like summary would answer specific questions, it could be retrieved. So could photographs of objects found at Delphi, articles discussing the political importance of the city and the temple, and the original Greek sources mentioning it. In this search for more information, the user would also be able to see a camera pan across the valley below Delphi or to compare how Plutarch used Thucydides as a source for his discussion and compare it directly with Thucydides' own presentation. At the same time, if what was needed was a listing of all the other sites in Greece having a type of pottery found at the Temple of Apollo (a more traditional database *retrieval*), that would also be available through Perseus.

DATABASES FOR PERSONAL NOTE TAKING

Commercial software applications are available that let individuals accomplish tasks very similar to those described above with their own information. The choice of which of these popular packages to use depends on how much you want to spend, how much time you want to invest in learning a new piece of software, and how complicated your data collection needs are.

At the simplest level, it is quite possible to use a word-processing program to take all the notes that one might ever need for any historical project. Instead of writing notes on note cards, those same notes can be entered into the word processor, with one *file* for each source or collection of sources. Because virtually every word processor includes a search option, it is a relatively easy process to look for particular information in each of the files. Someone studying the *Cahiers de doléances* of the French revolutionary period might create a series of Microsoft Word files, each one containing notes taken on a particular *cahier*. To find all the complaints regarding taxes, the user could load the files one after another, searching for any occurrence of the character string tax. Using the split-screen capability of the word processor, the text can be written with the notes appearing on the same screen.

This method, while having the advantages of not having to learn multiple pieces of software and facilitating the direct transfer of information from notes to text, has several disadvantages. The biggest of the disadvantages is that it is necessary to go through multiple files again and again to find particular bits of information. Although faster perhaps than re-sorting note cards again and again, reorganizing the material is not easy. For that reason, several companies are marketing different solutions to the problem of searching notes.

The first alternative is worth mentioning simply because it illustrates how new technologies can be used to recreate the original format. Some note-taking software packages like Squarenote include the option to print file contents on different-sized note cards. Word-processing packages can be formatted to print *output* to specially designed computer forms that serve as note cards. This approach creates more readable note cards. It also solves the problem of fading notes — those taken in pencil, as required by so many archives and special collections libraries. It does not really offer any improvement in organizing or finding the contents of those notes over the time-tested method of shuffling note cards in preparation for the writing process.

There is another approach to note taking that uses a software package to skim through all the files that contain relevant notes and creates an index to all the key words in the files. This makes the search for particular types of information easier and provides a ready reference tool, much like an index to a manuscript collection, for one's own notes. Because applications like Magellan search all *subdirectories* on a hard drive, these programs have the advantage of finding information that might be conceptually related even though the user stored them separately on the hard drive.

Each of these approaches to managing notes seems to offer significant improvements to the process of collecting textual materials for historical projects in terms of readability and ease of retrieval and access over pen-and-paper methods. Yet, they do not provide all the flexibility of full-text retrieval capabilities like those discussed above. To find that, one must turn to software applications that are designed specifically for that purpose. Such programs combine named fields and free-text in a way that makes note taking easy and retrieval of information flexible.

One such program, AskSam, is a good example of these possibilities. This program was used to take detailed notes on a series of scrapbooks collected by the Pullman Company that included clippings about the company, the town, its employees, and its business interests taken from newspapers throughout the world. Each article was treated as a document within the database. For bibliographic reasons, each of these documents contained three predefined fields: scrapbook (named BK), article name and newspaper (A), and page number (PN). Taking notes on the articles meant simply filling in each field and then typing the notes in whatever format seemed appropriate. In the process of taking notes, it became apparent that another field (named LOOKUP) would be useful for identifying additional sources that might be useful in the future. Eventually, notes were taken on all the scrapbooks, and the result was a 1.5 megabyte file—the equivalent of thousands of note cards.

Using the file is an easy process. To find citations about evictions in the model town, one need only select *query* from the *menu* and enter EVICT*. To find clippings from the *Chicago Inter Ocean*, all that is required is to specify OCEAN IN A, telling the program to look for the word Ocean in the field named A. To find articles discussing the issue of rights in Pullman, the query would be for the two words, rights and Pullman. The ultimate flexibility of the program became obvious later, when preservation needs required that an index of the scrapbooks be created for a microfilming project; the program made it possible to create that as well.

The Los Angeles County Historical Society has begun to use a custom-designed application called History Database, a very structured *text-oriented database*. This flexible program fulfills many of the Historical Society's database needs. First, it provides simple-to-use software that assists historians in collecting information and preparing it for use in writing. Second, because it standardizes certain elements of note taking, it introduces the possibility of creating a kind of archive of an archive. If historians later want to share their notes, an intermediate level guide to materials in various collections is available in machine-readable form.

Some of these text-oriented databases also work very well for collecting specific information that will be used later for a particular type of analysis. One project, for example, uses InMagic to analyze historical patient treatment records. Its retrieval and reorganization capabilities make it easy to find records of patients diagnosed with a given ailment and then to generate a demographic portrait of the group. Another project uses AskSam to create a massive biographical file of Cleveland lawyers in order to recreate educational, social, and political networks fairly easily.

Each of these various textual database programs has its own strengths and weaknesses. AskSam, for example, contains an entire programming language, has *hypertext* and graphics capabilities, and does numeric processing. However, many of these advanced functions are difficult to use. InMagic's ease of use is offset by its very high price. Oberon's DOS-compatible Notebook II Plus and its *Mac* compatible Bibliostax uses a combination approach similar to that described for AskSam, but is much stronger in terms of building bibliographic citations. Nota Bene, the Modern Language Association-endorsed word-processing program, contains a text-oriented database program within it. Its particular advantage is that it is a virtually seamless addition to the word processor. Its user has no need to learn additional commands or to move texts back and forth between the database and the written document that will result from the research.

Since 1987 when Apple began to market HyperCard with all its new computers, this piece of software has offered *Macintosh* users one way of organizing notes and bibliographies. The *stacks* correspond in function to databases; the fields described on the individual cards correspond to fields within the databases above. Finding a word or character string on any of the cards in the stack is as simple as pointing-to-find on the *pull-down menu* and entering the word to be located. The special strengths of HyperCard (and hypertext and hypermedia programs in general), that let the user link a particular card with *background* texts or graphics, impose some limits on its usefulness as a note-taking program. At the same time, they enhance its usefulness as a teaching tool, an issue that will be addressed in Chapter 5. HyperCard stacks exist for almost every imaginable topic, and many are available through *bulletin boards* and *public domain* distribution channels.

FIXED-FIELD DATABASES

The bulk of historical data collecting involves text. Some information sources are a combination of text and numbers; others are entirely numeric. For numeric structures, other software packages are more appropriate and easier to use for data collection than those discussed above. These other packages may be more appropriate because of the format of the source itself or because of the ways in which the information will subsequently be organized.

Good examples are manuscript census returns for the United States. For the census, fixed-field, structured database packages like dBASE, FoxPlus, Paradox, Rbase, Double Helix, and FileMaker might work best for historians. The original manuscript censuses for the late-nineteenth and early-twentieth centuries appear on pages as a grid of rows and columns. Each row represents one person, each column represents a particular type of information: address, name, relationship to head of household, sex, race, age, marital status, occupation, etc. To reuse the database terminology from above, each person represents one record; each column represents one field.

For the person interested in collecting census information, the first step would be to create a database in a package that contains fields of adequate width to store each of the columns on the manuscript census page. Each page of the 1900 census has a reel number, enumeration district, and page number for identification. Each person on that page has, where relevant, a line number and the appropriate information on address; dwelling number; family number; name; relationship to head of household; race; sex; birth month; birth year; age; marital status; indication of times married; children born and children still alive; birthplace; father's birthplace; mother's birthplace; year migrated to the United States; years in the United States; citizenship status; job; months unemployed in past year; months in school during the past year; whether he or she can read, write, or speak English; and whether the home lived in was rented, or owned and mortgaged, or paid off. Therefore, the database would have to have a field for each of those variables. For example, a field named REEL would be created that was four digits wide (because there are more than 1,000 but fewer than 9,999 numbered reels of census microfilm), where the actual number of the microfilm reel would be stored. Another field called NAME might be defined to be thirty characters wide, enough to include the longest name in the census. Three more fields named BP, PABP, and MABP, each twelve characters wide, would be where the birthplace information was stored.

Once the database was created, information from the census could be copied directly into the database. Many of these packages allow the data to be entered in either template or spreadsheet fashion, whichever is easier for the person entering the data. Not bound by the constraints of the earliest quantitative studies on *punch cards*, information can be entered into the database exactly as it appears on screen. Functions in the database program itself even allow the user to create new information such as Soundex codes for the individual entry. The programming languages built into the databases make it possible, for example, to create a household record based on the records of the household's individuals. If the database program is *relational*, information from one database can be joined with that in another. This means that if individuals are identified by enumeration district and family number in one database and another database contains one record of information on each family identified by enumeration district and family number, information from both databases are available to each other. These relational capabilities are particularly useful when collecting information from sources like employment records where, although every employee has the same kinds of records, the number of records an individual might have depends on how long he or she worked for the company.

Although the retrieval of information in these kinds of databases is restricted by the structure initially designed into the database, the retrievals are usually very simple and straightforward. To get a listing of the names, ages, and nativity of all the police in the 1900 census file sketched above would require, in dBASE or FoxPlus, that one only enter the command LIST NAME,AGE,BP FOR JOB="POLICE" or use the menu to accomplish the same thing. Moreover, because they have a predefined structure, moving the data into an *ASCII* file, a spreadsheet, or a word-processing file is equally straightforward.

SPREADSHEETS

Spreadsheets like Lotus 1-2-3, Wingz, Excel, and Quattro are the programs that convinced businesses that they should buy into the microcomputer market. Designed to do every kind of business accounting and forecasting possible, they, at first glance, seem to be an unlikely software prospect for historians attempting to gather data. For some kinds of information collection, however, they provide almost the perfect environment. Laid out like accounting sheets in rows and columns, these programs do arithmetic calculations almost immediately, make copying or moving from one cell (the intersection of a row and a column) or range of cells painless, and usually include translation facilities that transform spreadsheets to fixed-field databases of ASCII text files with little difficulty.

A source like a corporate payroll from the nineteenth century, an account ledger from the sixteenth century, or a tax roll from the twentieth century was most likely recorded using the same logic and format as these spreadsheet programs. In the case of the payroll, the names and the paycheck numbers vary from individual to individual, but very often the name of the department, the job classification, the hours worked, and the rate of pay do not. The fact that spreadsheets make it very simple to copy all the repetitive material eliminates much redundant entry. So, too, do the automatic calculation features built into a spreadsheet. For example, a payroll that gives an amount earned in piece rates, an amount earned in day rates, a subtotal for amount earned, deductions for stock purchases and wage advances, and a total for the paycheck can be preprogrammed to compute the subtotal and paycheck total by inserting formulas into the appropriate cells. Instead of having to type the amounts into the cells, one simply has to check to insure that the company paymaster did not make an arithmetic error.

OTHER POSSIBILITIES

The above discussion only begins to tap the possibilities for historians collecting information. Within our lifetimes, improvements in both software and hardware may change much of the nature of data collection. Imagine how the experience of conducting oral interviews might change if *voice entry* is perfected beyond its current levels. Even now, computers can be equipped with voice recognition boards that permit an individual to speak words and numbers into the computer. One can imagine a scenario in which interviewees would not speak into a tape recorder but into a computer. Transcription costs would virtually disappear, the contents of the interview would be immediately available to full-text searching, and, perhaps more intriguing, the interview could be played back again on a computer to hear the actual words as they were said.

Because photographic images are now readily transformable to high-resolution computer images, excellent-quality reproductions of such materials as medieval illuminated manuscripts can be stored in machine-readable form. Graphic and text *scanners* that take a document or an image and translate it into a format appropriate for a computer are falling in price and improving in accuracy. Physically entering information from sources like government publications or city directories might disappear as a time-consuming task if they can just be scanned into a computer to be analyzed. The lengthy task of note taking might be eliminated as journals, monographs, and primary sources become increasingly available in machine-readable form.

Options that five years ago did not exist or were outside the price range of most of us are now commonplace. What that suggests is that five years from now, the options that will confront us are hardly imaginable today. To take full advantage of what will develop, we as historians must consider not only how we will use those new tools to collect information, but how we might want to use them to analyze the information in ways that will advance our knowledge of the past.

III

*A*NALYZING *I*NFORMATION

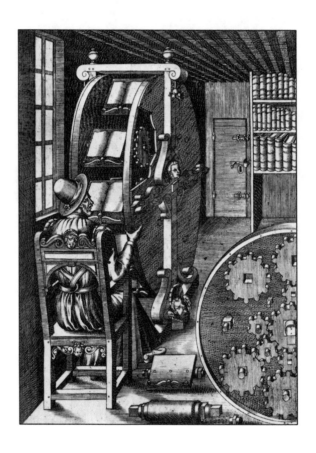

$

*T*he analysis of information stands at the heart of the historical process. Perhaps no other step is less standardized; in fact, it is the creativity of individuals in analyzing their data that makes history as engaging as it is. Despite the efforts of some of our best scholars to write about the process of analyzing information and crafting history, there is no single book or article that explains how to do it. Perhaps Carl Becker's title, *Everyman His Own Historian*, updated to reflect the current composition of those doing history, captures the ultimate reality of this phase of our work.[1] For that reason, it is unlikely that there will ever be an *expert system* that is able to mimic the intricate reconstruction of the past that historians do regularly in their writing or teaching.

Nonetheless, computers can facilitate historical analysis by doing what they do best — counting and computing, reorganizing information, presenting data in a wide variety of *formats*, pattern searching, simulating some historical situations and modeling others. Historians have, for more than thirty years, used computers to help them analyze historical data. Among the first to do so were the practitioners of the then "new" social and political history. Their reasons for using the computer were straightforward. The sources they used generated massive amounts of data that were awkward to manipulate by hand — sorting ten thousand note cards into stacks multiple times was simply too time-consuming to be practical. Once the data were put into *machine-readable* form, on the other hand, the computer could do whatever reorganization was required, in minutes, if not seconds. Moreover, many wanted to use statistical methods to analyze their data. Computing statistics by hand or by calculator is a tedious task at best. Computers, however, were designed to compute, and they could generate even the most complicated statistical measures easily, using software like SPSS or SAS. The fact that computers could eliminate much of the time spent doing almost mechanical tasks meant there was more time available for analysis and reanalysis. For these "quantifiers," the tool and the task were well matched — and the study of history benefited from the results.

With the advent of microcomputing and its wide availability, the dramatic improvement in graphics and text processing, the increasing sophistication and flexibility of *software*, and new levels of "user-friendly" technology, the possible matches between tasks and tools have expanded greatly. This chapter will explore some of the more interesting and generally applicable possibilities that have already appeared. To try to touch on all would be impossible. Those with very specific questions should consult the Resource Guide in appendix B, with particular attention to the journals *Computers and the Humanities, History and Computing,* and *Social Science Computer Review.*

LINGUISTIC, NUMERIC, AND QUANTITATIVE METHODS

One subject that has recently captured the imagination of many historians is language. Scholars of various countries, time periods, and political persuasions have begun to look at the power of words, their shifting meanings, and their importance for understanding the past. Few, if any, of these studies have used computers to analyze their texts in any systematic way. Yet, the use of computers in the related fields of literary criticism and linguistics is as developed as almost any field of computing in the humanities.[2] Computers have been used to analyze texts for authorship by comparing word choices and grammatical structures. Serious discrepancies between texts believed to be by one author point to the possibility that a second or third author might also have been involved. Through careful comparison with the styles of other writers, these analyses are also able to draw inferences as to who the other authors might be. Computers have traced the spread of words, phrases, and concepts through regions and language groups. They also have been used to emulate natural languages and for translation.

One example of the application of these literary and linguistic computing techniques to historical data is the work of Mark Olsen and Louis-Georges Harvey.[3] Interested in revolutionary rhetoric, they compared texts from the early phases of the French Revolution to a sample of French Canadian texts from the early nineteenth century to see first, whether the same language was used on both sides of the Atlantic, and second, whether the meanings of those common words were the same. Using a *personal computer* and a concordance program developed by Brigham Young University, Olsen and Harvey identified the *key words* in each set of documents and found a high degree of correlation between them.[4] However, an assessment of the words in context showed a very different pattern between the earlier French documents and the later Canadian documents. In the French texts, for example, the word *droits* was most often paired with the adjective *naturels* and the nouns *hommes* and *egalité*. The French Canadians were more likely to speak of their rights more concretely in terms of *droits et privilèges* resulting from their role as *sujets* and provided by the constitution. Words like *nation* and *pays*, *citoyen* and *sujet* reflected equally different usages and meanings. From that basic information, Olsen and Harvey could draw a series of conclusions about the nature of political discourse in the two linguistically similar but politically different cultures.

Such techniques might also be revealing for a number of other debates currently afoot among historians. One might envision a large text *database* of immigrant letters written from the United States to friends and relatives.[5] With the data, a careful researcher might look for discernible patterns in what men and women described as their experiences in America, the words they used, and the context in which they used them. If the letter collection spanned the centuries of immigration to the United States, it would be possible to see if America represented the same opportunities to those who came in 1720 as in 1920. If there were multiple letters distributed over the length of their residence from enough individuals, it would also be possible to ask questions about acculturation and how it manifests itself in both language and meaning. Similarly, consistency in the language and content of letters across national lines or the continued use of native concepts and words would illustrate the ongoing importance of the culture of the homeland — or the emergence of a distinctive hyphenated American consciousness. Such evidence might be useful for understanding the debates about republicanism, liberalism, and other ideological perspectives. In fact, were enough of these letters ever available, it might be possible to look at that intersection of gender, class, and race or ethnicity in a totally new way to see how each affects the basic ways historical actors have described their worlds.

The range of possibilities associated with the analysis of any historical texts is only beginning to be tapped.[6] It is, however, a wide-open field that will expand dramatically as software developers respond to the growing demand for text-processing tools. As more and more texts are put into machine-readable form by publishers and conservators, it will become increasingly easy for historians to take advantage of those tools. *Scanners* and related technologies will let historians apply those tools to the exact texts appropriate for their research. And, as a result of new texts, new technologies, and new questions, the computer can help historians in their quest for new answers.

Such has certainly been the case for those analyzing historical data numerically. Improvements in computer technology have made it possible to collect data in its original form instead of collapsing it into variables and categories designed to fit the 80-column *punch cards* and early versions of statistical packages required twenty years ago. A sharp awareness of the conceptual problems associated with those limitations attracted researchers with complicated data and questions to the *hierarchical* and *relational database* packages that now dominate database software. These packages provided the tools for reorganizing the data in a myriad of ways, each appropriate for a particular type of historical question.

For example, employment records have long held a special appeal for labor historians and others, while presenting a particular problem of organization and analysis. Whereas a short-term employee might have just one entry on an employment card indicating that she or he had been hired on one date, worked in one position at one wage rate, and left on another date to take another job, a long-term employee might have two hundred fifty such entries for promotions, furloughs, rates changes, strikes, and other such events. Earlier software constraints would have pushed the researcher to develop a single summary *record* that could represent both employees, as well as the others that had a number of job entries between the two extremes. That record might include information like the date of hire, the termination date, the first eight jobs held (if it appeared that most people had eight or fewer jobs), the last job held, the wage rates for each of those jobs and the date they began, the total number of positions held, the number of status changes in each of the decades the employment files covered, and other such variables.

The difficulties with such a record are immediately obvious. For people with more than eight jobs, much of their experience is lost. For those with only one or two jobs, the record contains much unnecessary information. Important information is also lost in the need to summarize and collapse. By counting the number of status changes in each of the decades, the researcher is able to see whether the work force was more volatile in one decade as compared to another. What is lost without a far more complex *coding scheme* is that the changes in the 1930s tended toward pay cuts, layoffs, and furloughs, whereas the changes in the 1940s tended toward rate changes and adjustments. Nor would it show the differences in how the actions were applied — the effects of seniority, unionization, and technological obsolescence might be lost.

With the more powerful databases of today, the researcher can enter all the data contained on the original records in their original form — a carpenter's job can be entered as "carpenter" instead of some numeric representation — and in their actual quantity. As suggested earlier, the database software permits reorganization and analysis of the data included in it. It also makes it possible to generate any kind of summary *record* or report. Depending on the analysis that is deemed appropriate, the database can create input records to a mapping package that show the residential distribution of employees by race, ethnic group, and job category. Or, it can generate records that can be used by a sophisticated statistical package to predict the likelihood that an individual will leave a job or be laid off. Or, it can print a listing of those workers not hired back after a strike so they can be followed in city directories or census manuscripts.

Many *text-oriented databases* now have similar capabilities. If the database's contents are well thought out and well designed, and if the database package has good numeric, date manipulation, and reporting capabilities, much preliminary analysis can be done within the database itself. For example, a database created for the purpose of collecting as much information as possible on individual members of the bar association in a particular city could be organized in such a way that the database could be used to generate a profile of the legal profession in that community over a period of time. Instead of taking notes using traditional note cards with one record (the equivalent of one set of cards) per source, the database could be established with one record for each attorney. Certain predefined fields such as year and place of birth, year entered the bar, year left the community or died, law firms, clubs, political affiliation, and education might be incorporated along with the notes and their sources into the individual's record. The inclusion of a numeric field with an assigned value of 1 on each record makes it possible to do quick counts of people and characteristics. Such a structure would not only let the researcher find the anecdote about the maverick attorney who threatened to strangle an uncooperative judge, but also would allow the researcher to generate a report on the demographic makeup of the local bar association in the 1920s, or a listing of the social memberships of the top law firms in the city. Like the more structured databases, the best of these text-oriented databases can also write out data to a file that could work as *input* into another piece of software for a different form of analysis.

For those interested in quantitative analysis, the choices available have expanded with the proliferation of statistical software packages that include new and more sophisticated statistical techniques, giving historians a wider range of powerful measures appropriate for their data and questions. Statistics especially developed for longitudinal data — data collected to include a time dimension — have freed historical analysis from the constraints of cross-sectional analysis that only allowed a comparison of data at one time with that of another time. Using available software, historians can now look at the timing of actual events and actions in the lives of individuals and nations instead of having to rely on fixed portraits on either side of the event.[7] Other programs bring a refinement to spatial analysis that former measures like the *index of dissimilarity* could not achieve. Not only can users measure actual spatial distribution of such things as people, goods, and services, they can also evaluate the mental maps people have of their environment.[8] Econometric programs permit the construction of complicated models using a variety of different types of statistics to analyze them. As statisticians devise and elaborate on various statistics that deal with the different data problems historians face, such as missing data, unequal population sizes, and value clustering, these statistics are incorporated into existing packages or turned into new software packages. For those with projects requiring computing resources beyond the capabilities of microcomputers, versions of the software are available on both the *mainframes* and even *super computers* available on most campuses.[9] Most of these packages, however, have been written or modified to take advantage of the things *microcomputers* do well — displaying data graphically and providing *menu-driven*, interactive analysis of the data. Even complicated analyses on large data sets can be done on personal computers.

GRAPHICS AND MAPPING CAPABILITIES

The graphics capabilities of microcomputers and the abundant graphics software available for them offer more options for those wanting to analyze their data visually.[10] Because historians are most familiar with the use of maps as a means for presenting data, the mapping capabilities of computers are a logical place to begin any discussion of visual tools. Although most cartographers would argue that computers still cannot draw beautiful maps, they can be used to draw quite adequate maps and, more important, to display all kinds of information within those maps with a certain amount of ease and with a great deal of flexibility. What is required to draw these maps by the computer is a set of coordinates that draws the map's outline, an optional overlay of geographic features, and the data to be displayed in the map.

One problem that has deterred historians from using computerized maps has been the fact that contemporary boundaries, the ones that are most likely to exist already in *digitized* form for computers, do not match historical boundaries. One solution to that problem is the various projects that are underway or have been completed that make historical boundaries available in machine-readable form.[11] Another solution has been to take advantage of a combination of *hardware* and software to create the maps individuals need for their research. Although expensive *digitizers* still provide the most detailed map outlines, inexpensive *graphics tablets* combined with *CADD (computer-aided drafting and design)* software, some *drawing* programs, or map-drawing programs specially designed to work with mapping software let individuals create and edit quite acceptable maps that serve as the basis for further geographic analysis and presentation.[12] They also make it possible to add the overlays of towns, rivers, roads, names, or whatever information that needs to be added to the map.

Once the maps are created using the units of measure that are required, the data can be organized to input into the map-drawing software. As long as careful thought was put into the unit of measure (that is, counties, nations, blocks, or houses) that divides the map, the information that is to be represented on the map and the format in which the data are to be displayed, almost any kind of map can be drawn. For example, William Cronon in his new book, *Nature's Metropolis*, uses SASGraph (a module of the SAS statistics package) to demonstrate the relationships between Chicago and its hinterland.[13] Myron Gutmann, in the project discussed more completely in Chapter 5, used Atlas software to illustrate the distribution of population and architectural type by house in particular communities.

The computerized maps above rely on actual geographic boundaries as their base. Computerized maps can also be used to determine boundaries. One dilemma that has always faced scholars doing community studies is what the community is. It would be possible using oral histories (or diaries or other kinds of descriptions) to reconstruct the boundaries of the communities based on the reports. Using the descriptions of community boundaries offered by the different respondents, it would be possible to overlay one image of the community on another to see where they overlap and where they don't. Moreover, it would be possible to see if men and women describe the community boundaries in the same way or if people who have jobs inside it describe the community the same way as people who don't.

One excellent example of how these maps can be generated and even published using computers appeared as an insert to an issue of *Historical Geography.*[14] In it was an ethnic map of Los Angeles and a description of the software used in creating it.[15] Data for the map were taken from a U.S. Census summary tape that provided the race and ancestry data using CENSPAC, a package designed to facilitate the retrieval of census data. Next, the data were run through a specially designed *FORTRAN* program to rank the data in the appropriate order. Then, the data were imported into Excel, a *spreadsheet* program where additional data were computed and fed into Map Maker, where the actual map was drawn. The map was then read by Draw It Again Sam, one of many drawing packages for the *Macintosh,* to add titles and other visuals. From there it was incorporated into a Ready, Set, Go file for *desktop publishing* and Adobe Illustrator to generate the over-lays to draw a color map. The result was an informative and attractive map of the ethnic distribution of Los Angeles' population.

The graphics capabilities of computers that are of value to historians are not limited to mapping. The range of different kinds of graphics software, from drawing programs to spreadsheets to specialized programs like Harvard Graphics to CADD programs, that can be applied to historical analysis is quite impressive. Tables and charts, once drawn laboriously by hand, can be quickly generated directly from data stored in a spreadsheet program, a database, or a statistics package. The ease with which the graphics are made once the data are available means that as categories are collapsed and expanded, as data are added, and as various interpretations are considered, the graphic representations of them can be generated on the computer screen, on paper, or even on slides or overheads almost immediately. It has become a relatively simple task to overlay different graphics presentations on top of each other in a way that can reveal historical change or unexpected differences.

The usefulness of superimposing one graphic on another as an analytic tool is not limited to graphics created to summarize information previously in another form. Such techniques can also be helpful for analyzing images themselves. With high-resolution graphics devices, digitized versions of the images, and specialized graphics software, computers can compare images and artifacts as easily as they compare words and numbers. Art historians and archaeologists have used them to trace the evolution of individual artistic styles and cultural changes as reflected in pottery and other artifacts. They have created image databases that are subsequently used to identify such diverse items as design patterns and coins.

Archaeologists have also been able to use the graphics capabilities of computers to display missing data. The same kinds of software that allow architects to design buildings allow archaeologists to recreate buildings on the computer from the pieces of foundation trenches, stones, and artifacts found at sites. Potsherds can be used to reconstruct pots. In fact, archaeologists can fashion possible models of whole settlements by drawing on a combination of materials found there, relevant information from other locations, and three-dimensional graphics software.[16]

INTERPRETATION OF DATA

This modeling of the past is not necessarily a complicated task with a computer. One of the most common pieces of software, the spreadsheet, can be used very effectively to explore possible interpretations of the past. Just as stock brokers take advantage of spreadsheets to project the value of portfolios or economists use them to predict the growth of the economy, historians can use them to evaluate different scenarios to explain how the economy, the population, or the electorate changed from one time period to another. Designed to combine mathematical formulas, logical testing, numeric data, and rapid calculations, spreadsheets are an excellent environment in which to investigate questions like those noted above. For example, demographers rely on life tables and a series of formulas to compute such basic rates as mortality and fertility. Because those rates are formulaic, a spreadsheet can be constructed to create the life table (and display it graphically as well) and compute those key demographic rates. Those same properties make it easy to use the software to predict what that same population would look like at the next census (or other accounting) to see if reality matched the prediction. If not, then the spreadsheet provides the computational power to experiment with possible reasons for the divergence by testing different patterns in births, deaths, and migration that might explain those variations. In fact, entire simulations looking both forward and backward can be built within these spreadsheets to help to understand the factors that contributed to making the past the way it was.

This chapter began with the observation that it might be impossible to create an expert system that duplicated the work of historians in analyzing information.[17] That does not mean, however, that such systems might not be useful to historians. It is not too difficult to envision, for example, a system that could complement the large number of historical projects currently underway throughout the western hemisphere and the world associated with the Columbian quincentenary. With some imagination and a great deal of time and knowledge, a historian or group of historians might be able to create a *knowledge base* that would approximate what was known in the old world at the time it first came into contact with the new.

The purpose of such a knowledge base and the expert system to utilize it would be to construct the intellectual world of Europeans in 1492 in a way that would permit those of us five hundred years later to understand the impact of the "discovery" of the new world, its people, and its bounty. The knowledge base would be similar in structure to those already constructed to identify oil fields, prescribe medicines, and diagnose computer hardware problems. It would store as many facts and rules for using them (such *links* as "if it doesn't rain the crops won't grow") from the late fifteenth century as could be gathered. It would also have to store information on the kinds of people who had access to that knowledge, because knowledge then, as now, was not consistently distributed throughout the population. Clever programming would make it possible to explore what kinds of responses groups and individuals would have to what was revealed to them for the first time in the years after 1492. The system could be fine-tuned by incorporating the actual responses that have been recorded.

Such a tool would serve several valuable analytic purposes. First, it would ask the developers to be very careful in defining the intellectual world of the late fifteenth century, paying close attention to who knew what and what they were able to do with it. To accomplish this, the project developers would have to draw from and consolidate the vast amount of research and interpretation already done by medievalists, Renaissance scholars, and early modernists. They would have to incorporate changes in the very concepts of knowledge. Just the process of collecting and encoding the information would reveal much about the world of 1492. Constructing the rules for using the information would be equally revealing about the assumptions we as historians in the late twentieth century impose on that world. Reviewing the results of applying such rules to a wider population and over a longer time period, it will be possible to evaluate interpretations from a broader perspective than simply our own research. Finally, by making such an expert system available to others to use and evaluate, the discussion about what we know about the European world and the impact of the contact with the new world on it could advance our own knowledge in any number of ways.

It is important to end this chapter with an observation on an issue that has probably entered most readers' minds by this point, the issue that fifteen years ago was expressed in terms of "garbage in, garbage out." The information presented here suggests that computers can be of real value in exploring historical data and interpretations. This is only true if the person who uses the computer is as careful in collecting and using information as she or he would be without the computer. Just as the computer can make it possible to see information in new ways, it can also encourage a kind of laziness that leads the user to accept the ways the computer does something without forcing the ideas, information, or software into other forms. It also raises the possibility of inappropriate applications that could produce misleading results. However, if historians use the technology with the care they normally bring to their sources, their interpretation, and their presentation of both, then the computer will serve historical analysis well.

IV

COMMUNICATING INFORMATION

⸹

$\mathcal{T}$he dramatic changes that have already occurred in the way we communicate information confront us daily. "Doonesbury" cartoons poke fun at the use of *fax* machines in the recent war in the Persian Gulf, but that technology has also invaded such diverse places as history department offices and Tiananmen Square. Some divisions of the National Science Foundation accept grant proposals through *electronic mail*, and *electronic publishing* is becoming more common in a variety of disciplines. The popular press contains articles about computers writing books and about students submitting videos of their assignments instead of papers. *The Complete Works of William Shakespeare* is available on *CD-ROM* as well as in leatherbound editions. People in Bloomington communicate almost instantaneously with people in Berlin using *BITNET* and *Internet*. Congressional hearings are viewed as they happen in political science classrooms via C-Span and campus cable links. Computer firms, *software* companies, and photoduplication services advertise their services, underscoring the critical importance of the visual presentation of texts and graphics for public appeal.

Many of our old assumptions about how ideas and information are communicated, how they are presented, and how long it should take them to circulate have been forever changed by the new electronic and digital technology. Historians are not immune to these changes. This chapter will explore some that have already occurred and suggest possible ways that even greater change might follow.

TERMINOLOGY: DEFINE AND CONQUER

For historians, the written word has been the most common medium for recovering past events and presenting them anew. We keep abreast of our fields through books and journal articles; we publish our finished work in the same fashion. Futures and reputations are made and lost on the quality of the final written project. It is no small wonder, therefore, that computers really made their first inroads into the historians' world under the guise of word processors.

With the help of Word Perfect, Microsoft Word, MacWrite, Nota Bene, Xywrite, or whatever personal favorite is selected, we discovered how easy it was to cut and paste on the screen as compared to using real scissors and glue. Editing manuscripts has become easy, at least from the standpoint of typing and presentation. A thesaurus is a *click* of a *mouse* away for anyone searching for the appropriate word. So, too, is the correct spelling of common words, which are stored in a dictionary that can be updated to include the words and phrases appropriate to a particular article or topic. With one or two keystrokes, one can emphasize a phrase by changing its size or **style**. "Clean" copies can be generated immediately, instead of taking hours, as with a typewriter. As a result, many historians, like other writers, now use *microcomputers* to manipulate their texts.

Most would argue that these technological innovations have not essentially altered the nature, process, or content of writing. Instead, they make it faster and easier to do those same tasks. Those who study writing and texts, however, are beginning to raise interesting questions about the ways these technologies are creating new possibilities and realities in both.

One of the possibilities of these new technological developments could be a move away from published journals and books, at least in the form we currently accept as standard. Scientists already use computers and electronic mail to report preliminary findings and to circulate information in a timely fashion, and some journals publish in both electronic and paper format. Eventually some of these will abandon the paper. As this happens, scholars will have to rethink their definition of a publication and make some serious decisions about which formats are most appropriate for which kinds of publishing.

For example, technological opportunities might lead us to adopt new forms of presentation for pedagogical purposes. Readers and document collections serve as a particularly good example of what is both a dilemma and an opportunity. Those directed at a student audience were created to give students an introduction to the interpretations of different historians or to provide a readily available collection of primary sources in one place. In either case, the other purpose was to make personal copies available to each student at a price that was more reasonable than if several different books had to be purchased.

Despite the best efforts of many individuals to create the ideal reader, the selection was never quite what any other instructor might prefer. Perhaps nothing illustrates that as clearly as the amount of instructional material that is distributed in photocopy form. Rather than send students to wait in line at the reserve desk of the library, faculty members send them instead to the local photoduplication center to buy bound packets that contain copies of the articles and documents compiled by the instructor. These meet the requirements of individual ownership at an acceptable cost and have the additional advantage of including materials especially tailored to the course. As legal issues begin to raise questions about the limits to and the expense of this service, it is again time to raise questions about the best forms for these collections to take.

Machine-readable documents may be a viable answer. One solution would be to scan the documents into machine-readable form and distribute them on a *floppy disk*. Most *high-density* floppies can hold a semester's worth of documents stored as text. Students can then read them on the screen, print them out on a printer, or import them into a software application package that lets students *search* the documents in ways that are easiest for them. This approach meets availability and cost standards; however, it does not solve the fair use and copyright issues now challenging photocopied packets.

Compact disk (CD) versions of books and journals might avoid those difficulties. Many campuses now experiment with a technology that allows users to indicate which disk they would like to use, such as *Dissertation Abstracts*, for example. A mechanical arm, much like one that selects a record to play on a jukebox, chooses the proper CD and puts it on a player that is accessible by the campus network. The information can be used from a library *workstation*, even if the user is in a dorm room or office. If all the books, journals, and manuscripts that might make up a reader were made available *on-line* or in CD-ROM versions by the copyright holders, then the need for such readers might eventually disappear. Students could just call up their reading assignments on their computer.

Still another possibility, which has been tried with some success at a number of institutions, is to develop an *optical disk* or CD-ROM that incorporates not only text but also the high-quality images that are often too expensive to include in the book version. Whether stored simply as text and graphics that can be individually retrieved or as elements of a more sophisticated *database* or *hypermedia* system (see the discussions in Chapters 2 and 5), this medium might eventually offer more in content for a lower price than a comparable reader.

Such a collection raises other important questions about how historians in particular and academics in general present their work. One critical issue is the definition of "publication." Does a reader stored on a compact disk carry the same academic prestige as a reader published by a major university press? Could it advance someone in rank or secure a candidate tenure? Is it subjected to different standards of evaluation than a printed version? Do, for example, photos, maps, and other images become critical elements of such readers when they appear in electronic form while they are largely excluded in print? Does annotation take on a new meaning in these collections because whole primary sources might be included instead of just citations? Do reviewers check the logic and detail of the *hypertext links* as well as just the selection of documents and photographs?

The existence of these materials in machine-readable form also raises the question of the final form of the text. One undergraduate described this dilemma in very understandable terms when he explained that word processors and floppy disks had raised fraternity paper files to a new level of usefulness. Cutting and pasting from different documents had become easy, as had changing the order of arguments. The thesaurus embedded in the word processor could easily give the document a very different tone by the judicious substitution of *key words.* By varying the layout on the page, any paper could also take on a new look. In fact, word processing had provided the means of eluding even the most diligent professor's quest to trap plagiarism.

Scholars, of course, present the problem in very different terms, but the key issues are very much the same. The first is the visual presentation of the text. Illuminated manuscripts helped readers with their task by using elaborate letters and miniatures that highlighted the text and provided visual images for the reader to use. Today's standard texts use neither of those devices. At best, authors are allowed to use **boldface** or *italics*.

Both the change to computer typesetting and layout and the emergence of alternate, nonprint media have opened new possibilities for presentation. *Unusual fonts can draw attention to particular points,* just as *digitized* images might free a writer from having to describe "belching smokestacks that covered all those who lived in Homestead with a layer of grime that seemed never to go away." Such innovations can and will change the relationship between author and text and text and reader.[1]

Equally important may be the question of when a text is complete. When the last *i* was dotted and the last *t* was crossed on a handwritten document, there was little incentive to change it. A manuscript that had to be typed with four carbon copies discouraged last-minute revisions, as did type that had already been set.

Now freshman writing programs boast that students work through ten or twelve drafts on their way to a quality product. Articles are sent to journals on floppy disks. It is no longer uncommon to receive final editing copy back in the form of the *output* from a word processor instead of page proofs. It is simpler to reedit a word-processor file that can be wholly incorporated into the *page layout program* to produce the final page than to completely reedit text that has already been typeset. Does the fact that even a "finished" product—one that has been published in some form—is stored in a *format* that can be edited, revised, and reused raise the specter that even a book might not be an author's final word?

NETWORKS, E-MAIL, BBS, AND OTHER TECHNOLOGIES

Other changes in how information is communicated have occurred as well. The use of *e-mail* is perhaps the most significant. To date, at least in the academic world, e-mail has been basically free, subsidized by institutions, computer and telecommunications companies, educational consortia, and government funds. Those wanting to use e-mail simply have to apply for an access account to the campus *host computer*. This user identification provides the security needed to use the campus computer and serves as the *mailbox* address where messages can be sent and responses received. This user ID, when combined with a school identifier, means that an individual can send and receive electronic mail from a growing number of other institutions located all over the world.

Academics were quick to see the advantages of these *wide area networks* like *Internet, BITNET, NetNorth,* and *EARN*. A message could be sent to Europe, without charge, which would arrive in the recipient's electronic mailbox minutes after it was posted. Because files could be transferred as well, joint authoring at a distance became much easier, as documents could be edited almost simultaneously. Electronic mail also became a convenient way to avoid playing telephone tag. And, for many, it developed into an arena for discussion and intellectual exchange.

These people also take full advantage of the electronic discussion groups that have grown up on these *networks*. The discussion groups are easy to create; all that is required is a host computer on which to maintain membership lists and to receive and forward messages, a *postmaster* to manage it, and some publicity to attract subscribers. The fact that they are so easy to create helps to explain their proliferation; the fact that so many people find them useful explains the rest. There are literally thousands of these electronic discussion groups available through BITNET and Internet. Anyone who is interested in a complete list can probably get one from the local campus postmaster.

Because the structure and function of these electronic seminars are basically the same, a description of one can be suggestive of how they are developing alternate channels of communication in the academic world. The Humanist electronic seminar (HUMANIST@BROWNVM.BITNET) was first established at the University of Toronto by a group of people interested in computer applications in the humanities. Drawing its initial subscription list from the membership of the Association for Computers and the Humanities and other interested parties, the Humanist became one of the largest of these electronic seminars. Now housed at Brown University, it offers humanists of all kinds the opportunity to discuss on-line whatever topics they want with other humanists throughout the world.

A subscriber to Humanist will receive what might seem to be an overwhelming amount of electronic mail. Notices of meetings of interest to humanists, especially those that have something to do with computer applications, are sent to all subscribers. So are calls for papers, job announcements, questions, and miscellaneous postings of general interest. These notices give subscribers easy access to

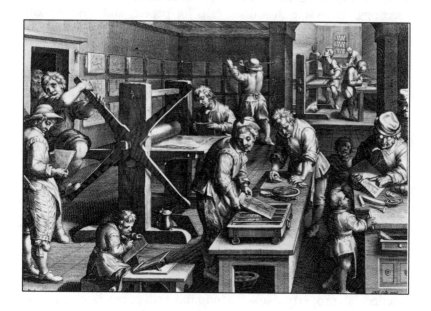

activities in a number of humanities disciplines. The ability to *post* questions lets a person on one campus find out what is happening elsewhere.

A subscriber can also join one or more discussion groups of people with common interests. These groups might reflect current political situations like the Persian Gulf War, pedagogical issues, or a particular research field. Discussions within the groups can be freewheeling and valuable. Some participants actually distribute early drafts of manuscripts; others use the discussion group to get early and informed feedback and interpretations as their ideas evolve. Individuals can enter and leave discussion groups as they like. For all these reasons, many people subscribe to the Humanist— and to any other of a number of electronic seminars.

The popularity of these seminars raises many interesting possibilities for the future. The first is their advantage for communicating timely information. Several professional organizations have developed their own electronic *bulletin boards* or seminars to facilitate the spread of information. One might imagine, for example, the existence of an on-line bulletin board for job openings in history. Departments would not have to worry about a possible month or more delay in the appearance of the job notice. Applicants would know immediately if the job search was canceled. Notices of meetings, fellowship deadlines, calls for papers, and other opportunities that have time-constraints would be perfect for posting on an electronic bulletin board.

Another possible use would be as a means to circulate papers. Most would agree that the quality of discussion about a presentation is almost always better if participants have a chance to read a paper as well as just hear it. In its early years the Social Science History Association, for example, tried to distribute papers as a way of making its conference sessions more useful to both presenters and the audience. Needless to say, the logistics of the distribution proved too difficult and the idea was abandoned. If the paper were posted on an electronic bulletin board, then persons who planned to attend the session could read it there. Someone who had to attend a competing session would still be able to read it and provide comments if they seemed appropriate. The value of attending sessions would be greater for all involved.

However, such a bulletin board would also present many problems that must be resolved. The first has to do with the issue of intellectual property. Now an unpublished paper is clearly the property of its writer. He or she does not have to provide copies to anyone, although typically papers are distributed to commentators and colleagues who request them. These copies almost always include some warning about reproduction or quoting. By knowing who has copies of the essay, the author maintains some control. Will that continue to be true if the essay is posted on an electronic bulletin board? Certainly *copy protection* schemes exist even now that could prevent someone from *downloading* the document. However, it would be available to anyone with access to the network. To protect its content, would the author have to declare a copyright at that point? If so, how effective would it be?

Closely related is the issue of what role the article as a publication form would have if written versions of essays were already widely available. Would there be refereed bulletin boards that would be the equivalent of publication (or perhaps simultaneous with publication) in a major journal? Or would there be a real need for articles if the exchange of information within disciplines was being conducted effectively through other channels?

Few professionals think these are issues that have to be resolved today. Yet, it is important for historians to keep the possibilities in mind. Publishers already devote a great deal of time and energy to considering the implications of the new technologies on their particular domain. What they decide will affect the form of and access to historical publications. Lawyers grapple with shifting definitions of copyright for intellectual works that take forms totally beyond the imagination of precedent-setting cases ten years ago. As new precedents emerge, changes might also occur in how we circulate historical information. Central repositories like the Inter-University Consortium for Political and Social Research might eventually distribute the results of research as well as the primary sources used to conduct it.

The nature of professional organizations also might be affected. Annual meetings serve a variety of functions: papers are presented, business is transacted, candidates are interviewed, and friendships are renewed and made. They provide an arena for intellectual exchange that few individual departments can provide. However, in a era of tight budgets and expanding communications choices, there might be increasing pressure to consider alternate strategies for achieving the same purposes. There are also questions about the centralization and nature of services provided. The success of many of these electronic bulletin boards and conferencing systems suggests how easily exchange between scholars can take place entirely outside organizational and national boundaries, a situation that was quite difficult even five years ago.

New communications technologies also raise questions about oral communication. No one will argue that they can be replaced by machine communications or that videotapes can replace instructors. However, there are new possibilities and expectations that may affect how we present and how we teach. Some have been suggested above; others will appear in the next chapter. One provides food for thought here.

On college campuses, in high schools, and in every project that involves a new library or museum, discussions take place about the classroom or the auditorium of the future. Debates over wiring possibilities and equipment choices occur—often without the participation of the instructors and lecturers who will use them. Many of us believe that the choice should be ours. Although we might insist on access to a video machine and a slide projector, we leave the computer links and graphics projection capabilities to the professors of science and business — the persons we assume will use them. That is an incorrect assumption.

Digitized texts and images taken from historical materials can be as readily viewed on desktop monitors and auditorium projection systems as can carbon models or quarterly profits. Imagine how much easier it would be for students to understand the structure of a medieval city if the instructor could lead the class on a visual walking tour of such a medieval city with high-resolution photographs so each student could see the display clearly. Using the computerized projection system, the instructor could *zoom* in to make a key point, then easily switch to a map to show the relationship of that city to its hinterland and other cities. Lectures might take on new forms, in either subtle or substantial ways. The kind of information conveyed might change. For some topics with less time needed for description, more time could be spent on analysis and discussion.

The next chapter will suggest how other possibilities might affect how we communicate historical data in one of the most important arenas, the classroom. Let us then turn to teaching history.

V

TEACHING HISTORY

§

$\mathcal{H}$istorians teach. Whether it is through their written work, as public history consultants, or in front of a classroom, historians devote a great deal of time teaching others how to understand the past.

Ten years ago, most teaching historians would have argued that computers had little, if any, role to play in history instruction of any kind. Only a few history teaching packages existed, primarily directed at elementary or junior high school students. Using a computer, a student could pretend to leave St. Joseph, Missouri, on a journey west on the Oregon Trail. Depending on hazards met along the way and decisions made by the student, the computer pioneers would reach Oregon or lose their lives along the way. Another student might assume the persona of the King of Sumer and have to make decisions that would affect the lives of every person in that ancient kingdom. Although these historical *simulations* captured the interest of many students, teachers, especially those at higher levels, worried that the programs were too simplistic and too little grounded in actual historical fact to play any central role in the history curriculum.

Another emerging type of instructional software promised little more. Drill and practice programs that served as electronic flash cards presented students with an opportunity to test their knowledge of historical facts and to practice what they didn't know. A question would appear on the screen that could be answered simply with a name, a date, or a yes or no. If the answer was correct, the program would congratulate the student and move on to the next question. If answered incorrectly, the question would be flagged and asked again later, or, in the better programs, the computer would offer additional information to help the student make a more informed response. These programs also came in for much criticism. History, of course, is more than facts. Even if these programs did provide a mechanism for mastering factual data, they offered little in the way of helping students conceptualize history. As a teaching tool for high school and college students, then, the value of the drills was limited.

Perhaps the only teaching application that generated any enthusiasm at the postsecondary level was in the same area computers were being most successfully used in research—in the quantitative analysis of social and political data. In classes entitled Quantitative

Methods in History and in courses where the faculty's own quantitative research seemed directly relevant, students learned SPSS or SAS on the campus *mainframe* computer while they learned measures of central tendency and studied the social structure of a French village or the voting patterns of the U.S. Senate.

INTRODUCING COMPUTERS TO CAMPUSES

Because quantitative analysis was the domain of so few historians, however, such instruction was rare. For the vast majority of historians, the possibilities of using computers effectively in teaching seemed as remote as using them in their own research. No existing piece of *software* provided a compelling example of why historians should invest their time or energy in developing *CAI (computer-assisted instruction)* materials for their own students. Nor did schools or colleges provide any encouragement, either explicit or implicit, for devoting the time required to integrate the technology fully into the instructional goals for a class.

In the mid-1980s that situation began to change. The accessibility of microcomputers as compared to mainframe computers contributed to the new enthusiasm. So, too, did the competition for the sale of microcomputers in the academic marketplace. Apple Computer had already come to dominate the elementary and secondary educational market in the late 1970s and early 1980s with its *Apple II* line of computers. Postsecondary academic computing was dominated by the big mainframe vendors, most notably IBM and Digital Equipment Corporation. The microcomputer market for colleges and universities was wide open.

When Apple introduced the *Macintosh (Mac)* in 1984, it also created the Apple University Consortium. This small group of prestigious universities was given substantial price discounts and the opportunity to work closely with Apple designers to develop instructional tools on the Macintosh and to provide input to Apple on ways in which Mac *hardware* and software could be made more useful in academic environments. Apple gave grants for hardware and programming support to the most imaginative projects proposed for using Macs in research and teaching. It published a magazine, *Wheels for the Mind* (now replaced by a newsletter called *Syllabus*), to showcase the results from these and other projects. Twice-yearly consortium meetings gave faculty members and academic computing personnel from all the universities a forum to present what they had accomplished and to learn what others were doing.

IBM was also active on this front. It lent machines to faculty members to use to develop teaching and research materials. Several universities received large grants for equipment, software, and systems development in IBM's Advanced Education Project program. IBM had its own magazines for the educational market and brought together different groups of academics to share ideas, products, and possibilities. Other vendors also entered the fray, but on a much smaller scale than either IBM or Apple.

The results of these efforts boosted sales revenues, but they were also important for developing a large group of microcomputer users on campuses and for creating a new awareness about the use of computers for instructional purposes. Some of the history software produced as a result of these efforts serve as models of what can be done with substantial resources. Among the earliest of these was a simulation package developed at Stanford University called *The Would-Be Gentleman*. The program was designed to be used in a course on the France of Louis XIV, taught by Carolyn Lougee. Using the package, students assumed the role of a "would-be gentleman" during the reign of Louis XIV. They had to make many of the same choices on the computer that an ambitious young man of the time would have to make—who his protector would be, when and whom he would marry, where to invest his money, and what positions he would be willing to take. Grounded in historical time, the student would find that a decision that was wise in 1648 might, literally, be fatal in 1690. If the fortunes of his protector, a real historical individual, fell, so might the student's. The more the student knew about the seventeenth century, French society, and politics, the better he or she would do in climbing the social ladder. *The Would-Be Gentleman*, winner of a National Center for Research to Improve Postsecondary Teaching and Learning (NCRIPTAL) prize for humanities software, dispelled the notion that historical simulations would always be more game than history. Instead it had become clear that, when well-conceived and executed, CAI could serve as a sophisticated teaching tool.

In a different area, the *Great American History Machine (GAHM)* proved that a computer could also serve as an excellent tool for helping students analyze primary historical sources. Developed under the guidance of David Miller at Carnegie Mellon University, where it continues to evolve, the *GAHM* combines maps with a vast array of nineteenth- and twentieth-century social, political, and economic data at the county level. Using the tools supplied with the software, students can explore that data visually and statistically to develop their own interpretations of ongoing historical debates. They can chart the spread of the population westward in America and then go further to ask what kinds of people (women or men, immigrant or native, farmers or laborers, old or young) led that migration. They can test the relationship between different types of agriculture and political party preferences. Designed to be used in conjunction with the American history survey course, the *GAHM* provides students with an accessible and flexible way to test interpretations offered in the classroom and in related readings by allowing students to substitute their own hypotheses.

CAI has been raised to an impressive level by the Historical Document Expert System Project (HiDES) at the University of Southampton, U.K. Caught by former Prime Minister Margaret Thatcher's cutbacks, which raised class sizes and cut resources, Frank Colson, David Doulton, and their colleagues looked for a way to give students the additional guidance they needed to complete their final-year requirement for the analysis of primary sources in their area of specialization. Their solution was an exciting computer-based system that used powerful application packages to create dialogues between students and sources to help students use those sources in an intelligent way. Within a HiDES, instructors can incorporate primary texts, numerical data, maps, and images with the *applications software* students use to analyze them. An individual HiDES project uses one of four approaches to walk students through the sources, depending on the instructor's preference. The "progressive" approach leads students through a logical sequence of possible interpretations. Another reconstructs a version of an event and asks the student to evaluate and criticize the reconstruction. The third creates an exposition from a major source, and the last asks the student to weigh the two sides of a debate. The HiDES prepares the students for their seminars and leads them to the library for more information. Equally important, it gives students a guided entry point to the primary documents of the topic available to them at their own convenience and pace. To date, more than twenty-four different HiDES projects have been built on topics as diverse as the European diplomatic crisis of July 1914, the Fifteenth Amendment to the United States Constitution, the abolition of slavery in Brazil, and the Second Battle of Antioch in 1098 C.E. Student and faculty responses to these HiDES projects have been positive. One very interesting result is that students who are using the HiDES seem, at least based on circulation statistics, to have increased their library usage.

These projects and others like them illustrate what can be done with the help of computer companies and institutions willing to provide release time, staff, or other support for the development of educational software. They also point to the directions historians might pursue if interested in using computers in their courses. Not everyone has to think in such grand terms, however. Computers can also be useful on a much smaller scale.

One problem that confronts every teacher is her or his availability to students. Office hours are often not convenient for students; late-night calls at home are not a satisfactory alternative. *Electronic mail* might be. Many campuses already have on-campus networks to which every student and faculty member has free access. Certainly, that access is enhanced if an individual has a computer and *modem* or other cabling in his or her dorm room, home, or office. Most colleges have computer labs that allow students who don't have computers to use that network. For pedagogical purposes, at the simplest level that means students can send their questions to their instructors whenever necessary, even at two-thirty in the morning. A faculty member can respond when convenient or arrange a time to talk with the student if the question defies a simple answer.

This communication can be made privately or on a class *bulletin board* on the campus network. The advantage to the bulletin board is that individual questions and responses can become *on-line* discussions. Students *post* their questons publicly and everyone in the class can see the instructor's answer and offer observations of their own. Students living on opposite sides of campus can discuss their readings and lectures through the computer or work on collaborative projects. Finally, a syllabus or assignment need never be lost because it can be posted on-line.

With the proliferation of community-wide *freenets*, like the one first developed in Cleveland, these communication possibilities expand even to the general public. The local library or historical society might establish its own bulletin board, and anyone with a computer, a modem, and a free account number may send in his or her questions about that community's history. If the question is specifically directed to the institution, someone on staff can provide the answer. Other questions can be directed toward the general public. For example, a question like "We're writing the centennial history of the Ravenswood Women's Club. Does anyone have any records of its activities that we could share?" might draw useful responses. One might argue that such usage is actually far distant.

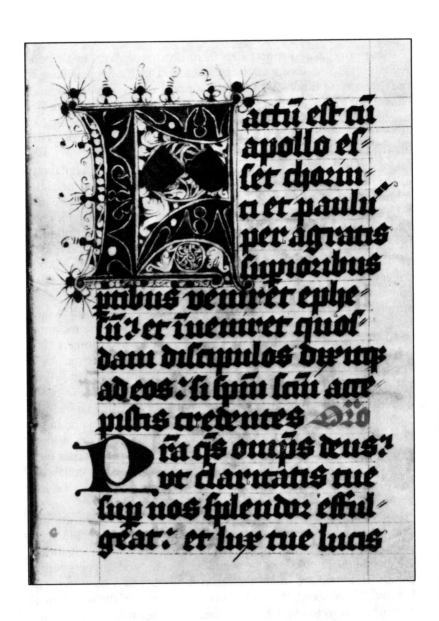

However, one large historical society willing to invest the staff time, combined with several active genealogical societies, can make a success of such a bulletin board very quickly.

Another area where familiar computer application might be used very successfully is in helping students understand the nature of arguments and the role of the author, both in their own writing and in the writings of others. Because most students now know how to use a word processor for editing, an instructor could use that knowledge to help them with larger issues. The massive literature on the use of computer technology in teaching writing is filled with exciting examples of how individual instructors are pushing students by taking advantage of *word processing*. One example will suffice here.

Students often have a difficult time understanding the importance of how language is used as an aspect of interpreting a historical document. To encourage this understanding, each student in a seminar might be given a document of some historical importance that is two or three pages long. It could be scanned into the computer so that each student would receive the document both on paper and on *disk*. Their assignment might be to edit the document to remove gendered language. Or it might be to take a description of an event and revise it to reflect the point of view of different persons who were there. The advantage of this approach over simply reading different accounts is that students become actively involved in the construction of the event or the document. Their finished results could be circulated to other class members, and they could use a class discussion to explain why they approached the topic as they did or why they chose the words they used. Such an assignment, made substantially easier with a word processor and its thesaurus, would help students understand firsthand the critical importance of language.

Spreadsheets are used very successfully in a number of history courses. The ease with which they can do calculations, their ability to do projections (both forward and backward), and the simple graphics they produce means that students, if given a well-chosen selection of historical data, can build their own models and test their own hypotheses. The effects of demographic factors are easier to see if students themselves build different population projections that vary age at marriage or number of children born. Household budget data across time and across countries can be adjusted for inflation, regrouped into categories of the student's own choosing, and presented graphically in ways that let students see both cultural choices and economic constraints. One imaginative instructor has students use spreadsheets to refigure tables in history textbooks and construct alternate graphs and interpretations. Such examples show that spreadsheets can be a valuable tool in helping students grapple with virtually any historical question for which there are appropriate numeric data.

Many historical questions, however, cannot be answered by numbers or with numbers alone. For those questions, instructors might want to turn to other popular software such as *text-oriented databases*. By incorporating historical documents, they can be turned into powerful teaching resources.

For example, virtually every class on revolutionary America devotes some time to the debates that preceded the ratification of the Constitution. Very often, the *Federalist Papers* are used as readings for this section. Those papers are now available in *machine-readable* form. The possibility exists, therefore, that a vendor could market these documents with a *database* program, or that an enterprising faculty member could import a copy of the *Federalist Papers* into a suitable database program. Because the *key word searches* would provide students with immediate entry points to all of the papers, students could be expected to use them to explore all kinds of questions critical to the formation of the American state. With one command, every use of the word republican could be called to the screen. Through a careful reading of the text, students could begin to understand the assumptions of this important American political concept. If students had access to a comparable database of anti-Federalist writings, they might also begin to see how the nature of these key concepts were contested.

Hypertext programs are another effective teaching tool. Because they let instructors annotate materials and suggest logical *links* to other documents and resources while not restricting students to that approach, they have become very popular, as indicated by the number of HyperCard *stacks* already available. Envision a hypertext file that contains all the treaties ever signed by any Native American tribe and the United States government. The instructor building the file would be able to annotate each treaty in ways that would be quite helpful to the students. The name of each tribe could be linked to a general description of its history. Another link might provide a description of the economic and social conditions the tribe faced at the time the treaty was signed. The file might also include a description of the historical impact of the treaty — from the perspectives of the American Indians and the U.S. government. By *clicking* on the location where the treaty was signed or the description of the lands discussed in the treaty, a student could call up a map on the screen or a description of the natural resources found there. Such a hypertext file could evolve into a wonderful reference source for students and could be used in a number of different history courses.

The possibilities associated with either these text-oriented databases or hypertext are not limited to the classroom. Many museums are currently considering ways to construct publicly accessible databases that would contain individual histories and reminiscences. These databases would serve a function similar to oral history archives but would be much more accessible. Instead of (or in addition to) having people record their stories on tape, they would be entered into the computer. This database would then be available to museum visitors as a way of learning more about what it was like to have lived in that neighborhood, worked for that company, or whatever the focus of the database might be.

Such an implementation in a local history museum might mean that the current resident of 1049 W. Taylor could do a *query* on that address and find out who lived there in 1904 and 1935. A person who had just seen an impressive piece of machinery on display in the museum could type in its name and find out what someone who had worked with the machine had to say about it. As the database grew, it would become an increasingly important archive for the museum, the community, and the scholars, who would find it an incredibly rich source.

Hypermedia takes this notion one step further to include video and audio. The success of the recent PBS series, *The Civil War*, provides insight into how these multimedia systems might enhance teaching. In the series, photos, music, and historical analysis were combined in a way that captivated audiences while imparting important historical knowledge. Hypermedia incorporates all those same options and possibilities into a computer application. Such a project, The Civil War Hypermedia Project, is currently under development at George Mason University. It includes a *videodisk* that contains many of the Civil War photos used in the series. The popular songs of the day will be encoded to be played back as the student chooses. Also central to the system will be a collection of Civil War documents taken from such sources as newspapers, diaries, and government publications. There also will be articles written by historians that lay out critical debates on the war and its meaning and implications.

Each of these parts can be located or searched independently, or they can be traversed according to the predefined links. A student could combine the investigation of an ancestor who fought at Gettysburg with general information about the battle. The student would first call up photographs of the battle and the reports describing it to find out more about where and how the ancestor died. The student could then use the system to scan family photographs and enter details from family letters and journals, perhaps to develop a paper relating his or her ancestor to the Civil War.

Another student might begin by reading the assigned article on the origins of the Civil War stored in the *file*, then jump immediately to several of the primary sources cited in the article, which are also part of the file. Curious as to whether other commentators might have another interpretation, the student could search the text for the word origins or some equivalent phrase, or go to the library to find several other sources cited but not included in the file. This student would also work through the material in search of an individual interpretation.

Similar collections also are beginning to appear. A French Revolution collection that takes advantage of videodisk technology, although not the complete hypermedia approach, is already being marketed. Organizations such as IRIS at Brown University have created impressive hypermedia systems in related disciplines. The Center for Instructional Technology at the University of Southern

California is developing instructional materials like Project Jefferson that show the power of hypermedia applied to historical data. And the Perseus Project described in Chapter 2 promises to set a very high standard for systems like it.

Here the skeptic can raise the question as to whether these packages in particular or the use of computers in general is anything but glitz, a trendy addition to classes that takes more time away from the real business of teaching history than what it adds. To those who remind us that today's students are unique products of a television and video age that require new methods of teaching, as historians we can respond that seventeenth-century observers rued the fact that students then also greatly preferred images to words. Yet, evidence does exist that at least some classes that incorporate computers have been very successful in teaching history and historical methods to students.

An honors seminar at the University of Texas provides a good example of the kind of success that can be achieved. In three consecutive years, students in this seminar relied heavily on microcomputers and software packages like dBASE, Atlas, and SAS to help them re-create the population of two Texas towns, Fredericksburg and Lockhart. Individual students in the class were able to produce high-quality honors essays on topics of their own choosing based on the combined data collection efforts of the seminar. The data collection software developed for the class is now available to other instructors and researchers who might want to use it. In addition, several articles have already been published using the data from the class. These students were clearly involved in the process of serious historical research and writing, a goal that is often hard to achieve, even in classes that do not use computers.

The Texas project is illustrative of another point, however. The professor who designed the class, Myron Gutmann, has been quick to point out that the use of the computers came at a high overhead. This a common factor among those who use computers as an aid to teaching. Expenses can come in the development of software; one successful project estimated that it cost approximately $50,000 to complete. That amount, however, paid for a piece of software that needs virtually no explanation or computer instruction. For those who use off-the-shelf software, there is the ongoing cost of faculty time spent answering computer questions. Most colleges or universities have yet to resolve the dilemma of providing computer consulting or instruction for the varied computing applications and needs of a diverse body of users. Despite the advantages of *graphical user interfaces,* students still have difficulty understanding the logic of individual programs.

Designing instructional computer applications also requires huge amounts of faculty time in conceptualization, data collection, and implementation. It is probably safe to argue that such efforts take at least as much research and organizational time as one journal article, if not more. One of the issues that surfaces at every meeting devoted to academic computing is the fact that there is generally no reward system for individuals who develop instructional software. Although the development may result in an annotated collection of sources as elaborate as a published volume that may be distributed through the academic software clearinghouses, it is not likely to carry the weight of an article in even a lesser journal. At best, it will be considered as evidence of a commitment to teaching. This belief has helped to create a system where humanists, who are probably less likely to use computers in their own research, have also been less likely to pay the heavy costs in developing instructional software or data files that can be used for teaching.

This does not have to be the case. In institutions where such efforts are encouraged, high-quality humanities and history software is being developed, as the packages noted above and many more than are listed attest. The best of these have also received an EDUCOM/NCRIPTAL Higher Education Software Award. As it has since the mid-1980s, in 1990 this group awarded prizes for the best software in various academic disciplines. EDUCOM/NCRIPTAL also gave awards for the best curriculum innovation in the humanities, for a large class, and in a laboratory.

The fact that exciting pieces of academic software like these prizewinners exist points to what might be done by combining computer technology and the study of the past. As changes take place in how research is conducted, how results are published, and how the public, both inside and outside the classroom, prefers to receive information, then historians will, like others, find themselves using these technologies in ways not yet even contemplated.

EPILOGUE

§

*D*uring the weeks this pamphlet was being readied for publication, a number of significant changes occurred in the arena of information technology. IBM and Apple announced that they would begin to discuss some joint efforts, possibly helping to bridge the chasm between the two styles of personal computing. WordPerfect announced that it would incorporate a *graphical user interface* in its next version. And, on a recent radio talk show, the editor of a new collegiate dictionary discussed what the electronic dictionary of the future could be and how quickly it will arrive.

Although none of those single events will immediately change the way we historians do our work, each suggests that eventually such events will affect our work — perhaps in small ways, perhaps in ways so profound that we cannot even predict what they might be. Some changes will be welcomed; some will not. Many changes will be unavoidable.

What this volume has tried to do is to show how certain aspects of this technological revolution can and will affect our professional efforts. It has tried to suggest ways that we can use *hardware* and *software* as tools to help us become more efficient historians. It has also tried to suggest that the computer may ultimately transform the way we perceive and perform our work as historians.

If the pamphlet has been successful, it has raised the possibility that most historians can take greater advantage of the technology than they have so far. Ideally, it has provided enough information to convince most readers that computers are neither so difficult nor so inappropriate to the historical process that they should be avoided — but rather that the overview offered here may challenge readers to make the technology their own.

In making the technology our own, we can help to shape it, to set its directions in the areas that most immediately influence our work, whether in collecting, analyzing, communicating, or teaching historical information. It is important that historians do this. If we abdicate our role in making these decisions to those who understand computing but who do not fully appreciate its potential impact on the kinds of teaching, research, and writing we do, then we run the risk of seeing the technology structure the way we do our work. There is no reason for this to happen. If we can be as creative in approaching our work with computers as we are without them, then computing will become an important part of the way that we practice our craft, and we will all benefit from its inclusion.

Janice L. Reiff
Summer 1991

ENDNOTES

Preface

[1] For a compelling call for our participation, see Marilyn Schmitt, "Scholars Must Take the Lead in Computerization in the Humanities." *Chronicle of Higher Education.* November 21, 1990.

[2] Robert Darnton. "A French Inspector Sorts His Files," in *The Great Cat Massacre.* (New York: Basic Books, 1984).

Chapter I: Structuring the Past

[1] Bolter, Douglas. *Turing's Man.* Chapel Hill, N.C.: University of North Carolina Press, 1984.

[2] This is not to argue that compact disks will necessarily replace trips to archives and research libraries. Clearly too much would be lost in ambience and intellectual exchange.

[3] Glick, James. *Chaos: Making a New Science.* New York: Penguin, 1987. Glick has provided the most easily accessible introduction to chaos theory. For an application of chaos theory in a related discipline, see N. Katherine Hayles, "Chaos as Orderly Disorder: Shifting Ground in Contemporary Literature and Science," *New Literary History* 20 (Winter 1989): 305–22.

Chapter II: Collecting Information

[1] Crane, Gregory. "Challenging the Individual: The Tradition of Hypermedia," *Academic Computing* 4 (January 1990): 34. The discussion of the Perseus Project in this chapter derives heavily from this article. For more information, see also David L. Clark, "Computer Database Management for Historical Research and Writing," *Perspectives* 29 (April 1991): 10–12.

Chapter III: Analyzing Information

[1] Becker, Carl. *Everyman His Own Historian.* New York: F. S. Crofts & Co., 1935.

[2] The Association for Literary and Linguistic Computing and its journal provide the clearest reflection of this computer use.

[3] "Computers in Intellectual History: Lexical Statistics and the Analysis of Political Discourse," *Journal of Interdisciplinary History* XVIII (Winter 1988): 449–64.

[4] To measure the correlation, Olsen and Harvey relied on the work of Maurice Tournier, "Le vocabulaire des pétitions ouvrières de 1848: étude des parentages statistiques" in Régin Robin, *Histoire et linguistique* (Paris, 1973), 261–303. They also found a correlation between both of their keyword lists and that of Tournier.

[5] See Michael Ray Wood and Louis A. Zurcher, Jr., *The Development of a Post-Modern Self: A Computer-Assisted Comparative Analysis of Personal Documents* (New York: Greenwood Press, 1988).

[6] For another interesting example, see Stana Nenadic, "Identifying Social Networks with a Computer-Aided Analysis of Personal Diaries," in Evan Mawdsley, Nicholas Morgan, Lesley Richmond, and Richard Trainor, eds., *History and Computing III: Historians, Computers and Data* (Manchester, U.K., and New York: Manchester University Press, 1990).

[7] See, for example, Karl Ulrich Mayer and Nancy Brandon Tuma, eds., *Event History Analysis in Life Course Research* (Madison, WI: University of Wisconsin Press, 1989). This is, of course, a data availability problem as well as a statistical problem. Census data, for example, have to be analyzed for the type of data they are.

[8] Both SPSS and SAS generate these measures.

[9] For more information on supercomputing applications, see Vernon Burton and Terence Finnegan, "Supercomputing and the U.S. Manuscript Census," *Social Science Computer Review* 9 (Spring 1991) 1–12, among other articles.

[10] Tufte, Edward. *The Visual Display of Quantitative Information* (Cheshire, CT: Graphics Press, 1983) and *Envisioning Information* (Cheshire, CT: Graphics Press, 1990).

[11] For example, the County Historical Boundary Project done at the Newberry Library and available as ICPSR data set 9025 permits the re-creation of county boundaries for fourteen states at any time from 1790 to 1980. Another collection of historical county outline maps was done by Thomas D. Rabenhorst and Carville N. Earle in the geography department at the University of Maryland, Baltimore County. Contemporary maps of America at very detailed levels and of other countries are available through a variety of different vendors.

[12] For a review of this software, see L. Douglas Kiel, "Thematic Mapping With Microcomputers: Graphic Display of Social Scientific Data," *Social Science Computer Review* 6 (Spring 1988), 197–209.

[13] Cronon, Willliam J. *Nature's Metropolis: Chicago and the Great West*. New York: W. W. Norton, 1991.

[14] *Historical Geography* 19 (no. 2, 1989) —.

[15] A more complete description appears in Gene Turner, "Production of Ethnic Map Patterns in Los Angeles," *Occasional Publications in Geography* 5 (1989), Department of Geography, California State University, Northridge.

[16] Computer technology has had a significant impact on archaeology. For a brief introduction, see the 1990 issue of *Science and Archaeology* (vol. 32), "Communication in Archaeology: A Global View of the Impact of Information Technology" and the *Archaeological Computing Newsletter*.

[17] Not all would agree with that contention. See Caroline Bourlet and Jean-Luc Minel, "From an Historian's Know-how to a Knowledge Base: Using a Shell," in Mawdsley, et al., *History and Computing III*, 55–59.

Chapter IV: Communicating Information

[1] Richard A. Lanham. "The Electronic Word: Literary Study and the Digital Revolution," *New Literary History* 20 (Winter 1989): 265–90.

Appendix A: GLOSSARY

This glossary contains the terms that appear initially in italics within each chapter of the text. In addition, some background terminology is included with regard to computer hardware, software, and functions. Whenever possible, technical terms used within definitions have also been listed.

16-bit — Reference to amount of data processed at one time. A 16-bit data bus transmits 16 bits (2 bytes) at one time. A 16-bit computer uses a 16-bit data bus and processes information in 2-byte units.

32 bit — Reference to microprocessors and buses that process information in 32-bit segments. A true 32-bit computer uses a 32-bit bus both internally and externally.

8086 — Microprocessor introduced by Intel in 1978. What distinguishes this chip from the 8088 is its 16-bit data bus structure.

8087 — Numeric coprocessor designed to work with 8086 or 8088 microprocessor. This support chip allows the computer to do mathematical calculations much more quickly.

8088 — Microprocessor introduced by Intel in 1978. Although the chip has an internal 16-bit data bus structure, it communicates with its peripherals using an 8-bit data bus. This was the chip that powered the first IBM Personal Computers and clones.

68000 — Microprocessor introduced by Motorola that uses an internal 32-bit data bus and a 16-bit external data bus. The chip can address 32 gigabytes of random-access memory (RAM). This was the chip used in the first Macintosh.

68020 — Motorola microprocessor that uses a full 32-bit architecture and can address 32 gigabytes of RAM. This 16-MHz chip doubles the speed of the 68000.

68030 — Microprocessor developed by Motorola that uses a full 32-bit data bus, runs at higher speeds than either the 68000 or 68020, and includes special virtual memory management features.

80286 — Microprocessor introduced by Intel in 1984. It uses a 16-bit data bus and can address, in its protected mode, 16 megabytes of RAM. This was the chip that powered the IBM AT and clones.

80287 — Numeric coprocessor designed to work with 80286 microprocessor.

80386 — Microprocessor introduced by Intel in 1986. The 386 uses a 32-bit data bus and can address up to 4 gigabytes of memory. Among its other advances over earlier chips is its ability to divide memory into 640k blocks so that several DOS applications can run at the same time under software such as Windows or Desqview.

80386SX — Microprocessor introduced in 1988. This chip shares all the internal characteristics of an 80386 but communicates externally using a 16-bit data bus. This allows computers using this chip to take advantage of the less expensive 16-bit peripherals.

80387 — Numeric coprocessor designed to work with 80386 microprocessor.

80486 — Microprocessor introduced by Intel in 1989. This chip uses a 32-bit data bus and can access up to 64 gigabytes of memory. In addition the functions of the numeric coprocessor have been incorporated into the chip itself. The 486 chip includes over a million transistors on its silicon chip.

A

access time — Length of time between when the operating system issues a command for data retrieval and when the disk is able to transfer the data. This information, usually given in milliseconds (ms), is used to describe disk drive performance. When using large databases or manuscripts, the difference in amount of waiting time between a fast drive (e.g., 12 ms) and a slow drive (80 ms) can be substantial.

adapter — Electronic circuit board that fits into a computer's expansion slots.

ADB — *Apple Desktop Bus*. This is the standard interface for connecting input devices (mouse, keyboard, trackball, etc.) to the Macintosh SE and later Macintosh models. The ADB has been described as a single-master, multislave serial bus. In this description, the Macintosh is always the master; the multislaves are the keyboard, mouse, and other input devices daisy-chained together.

AIX — Version of Unix operating system developed by IBM for certain of its computers.

ALU — *Arithmetic/Logic Unit*. This is the section of the CPU (central processing unit) where the computer executes the arithmetic and logical operations.

Amiga — Personal computer developed by Commodore International. Based on Motorola's 68000 chip, the Amiga has arguably the best graphics and sound of any of the microcomputers. The lack of application programs for business and education that run on the Amiga has limited its widespread use.

analog — A continuous representation or signal, distinct from digital representation, which is composed of discrete elements. A seismograph that continually records the earth's movement is an analog device. So, too, are the signals over a telephone line.

analog/digital adapter — Adapter that allows a digital computer to accept analog signals. These converters are widely used in scientific and lab applications.

animation, computer — The use of a computer to create the illusion of movement by displaying slightly different images one after another.

ANSI — Acronym for American National Standards Institute. The Institute is an organization that works to set voluntary standards in a variety of industries, including the computer industry.

ANSI.SYS — A configuration file in DOS and OS/2 required by some applications to display the information according to the ANSI standards. When required, the instruction appears as the statement DEVICE=ANSI.SYS in the CONFIG.SYS file.

anti-virus program — A specially designed program to isolate and correct a computer virus found on a computer disk. These programs are often also called vaccines.

Apple Desktop Interface — User-interface guidelines developed by Apple to insure a consistent appearance and interface by all applications written for the Macintosh.

Apple II — Apple Computer's 8-bit personal computer. These computers helped create the microcomputer revolution. They are still widely used in public schools throughout the United States.

AppleShare — Apple's network operating system that lets a Macintosh work as a file server on an AppleTalk network.

AppleTalk — Apple Computer's local area network, able to link up to thirty-two devices. Using a bus topology and the AppleTalk port on every Macintosh, AppleTalk can also connect IBM-PC–compatible computers that have been fitted with an appropriate adapter card.

application programming interface — Special set of standards for use in a particular operating system that makes all applications have the same look and feel or end-user presentation interface.

applications software — General term for computer software programs designed to accomplish a specific kind of task. Examples of application software include word-processing, spreadsheet, communications, and database programs.

argument — The information following a command that tells the command on what it should act. Synonymous with parameter.

Arpanet — Early network supported by the U.S. Department of Defense Advanced Research Projects agency to assist in scientific research.

artificial intelligence — Research area devoted to the relationship between computers and human intelligence. To date, this research has focused on certain areas such as natural language processing, robotics, and expert systems.

ASCII — Acronym for American Standard Code for Information Exchange. Standard computer character set designed to facilitate the exchange of information between different kinds of computers and different types of software. The standard ASCII character set contains ninety-six upper- and lower-case characters and numbers and thirty-two control codes. Because this set does not allow for graphics or most non-English letters, most computers now use an extended character set that incorporates those as well.

ASCII file — Computer file consisting only of characters that appear in the ASCII character set. Such files are commonly used to transfer information from one hardware or software system to another.

aspect ratio — The relationship between the horizontal and vertical dimensions of a graphics image.

asynchronous communication — Method used to transmit data in the form of continuous bits marked by a start-and-stop bit that lets the receiving machine know how to read the input. This is the common form of data transmission used to communicate over telephone wires.

A/UX — Apple's version of the Unix operating system designed to run on the Macintosh.

B

background — Area of computer multitasking environment where low priority activities can execute at the same time another application is being executed in the foreground. Tasks like printing and downloading are common background processes.

backlit display — Type of liquid crystal display (LCD) that provides lighting from behind the display to improve readability.

backup — The most important responsibility of any computer user. All important information stored on a computer, whether programs or data, should be copied to another (backup) floppy disk, cartridge, tape, or other removable storage device in case something happens to the original storage medium. Making this safety copy can be done simply by copying files from one device to another or by using a backup utility especially designed to facilitate the transfer of data from a hard drive to some other medium, like floppy disks.

bandwidth — A communication channel's transmission capacity, reported in bits per second (bps).

batch file — A file containing a series of commands that will execute sequentially. Probably, the most common batch file in personal computing is the AUTOEXEC.BAT file that automatically runs each time a DOS-based computer is turned on.

batch processing — Method of computer operation where the computer executes programs and instructions without user intervention, usually contrasted to interactive processing. Often associated with large multiuser systems, batch processing can also be useful on microcomputers for running time-consuming tasks that do not require user intervention.

baud — Measure of the speed of a communications channel given in number of times per second a change in electrical state can occur.

baud rate — The speed at which asynchronous communication takes place. At low speeds such as 300 baud, this usually represents a transmission rate of 300 bits per second (bps), but at higher speeds the bits sent per second usually exceed the baud rate. Modem speeds are usually defined in baud rates, with 1200, 2400, and 9600 baud currently being most common. Often serial printers must also be configured to a particular baud rate.

Bernoulli box — Removable cartridge storage system developed by Iomega Corporation that works with both IBM PC-compatible and Macintosh microcomputers. The technology is named for the seventeenth-century Swiss scientist who studied the dynamics of rapidly spinning flexible disks around a fixed object.

bibliographic retrieval service — On-line service that provides access to bibliographic indexes and, increasingly, to full-text.

binary file — File containing information in format other than that of a text or ASCII file. These files are often stored so they can only be read by a particular piece of software or on a particular computer. Special protocols are often necessary to transmit the file over communication channels.

binary numbers — Base 2 number system utilizing only two digits (0,1). Most computers rely on the binary number system because it can be represented so easily by electronic circuits that recognize only two states (high current and low current).

BIOS — Acronym for Basic Input-Output System. Programs encoded in a computer's ROM that control the transfer of data and instructions between the computer and its peripherals. These programs are part of the computer's firmware.

bit — BInary digiT, the smallest piece of information a computer can use. The electronic representation by low or high current of one of the two binary digits (0 or 1).

bit map — Computer representation of an image. Each pixel (picture element) of the image is stored in a bit (or a series of bits for color and gray scale images).

bit-mapped font — A font for screen or printer that builds individual characters from a pattern of dots.

bit-mapped graphics — Images created from a series of bits, each mapped to a single dot on the screen or input device. Unlike object-oriented images, the output resolution of bit-mapped graphics is limited by the input device, regardless of the potentially higher resolution of the printer. Many paint programs and scanning devices generate bit-mapped graphics.

BITNET — Acronym for Because It's Time NETwork. A computer network created by EDUCOM to improve scholarly communication, particularly in the areas of electronic mail and file transfer. Access to BITNET requires an identification name or number provided by an institution that has an address on the network.

block — In word processing, the highlighted section of text that can be reformatted, deleted, copied, or otherwise manipulated. In communications, the unit in bytes that is transferred from one computer or device to another. In operating systems, a group of bytes linked together for performance reasons.

block graphics — On IBM PC-compatible machines, graphics created on the screen using the extended character set.

block operation — In word processing (and some other programs), operations involving a segment of text or information. The most common of these operations are moving, copying, deleting, and formatting.

Boolean logic — Type of logic developed by George Boole, a nineteenth-century British mathematician. Simply stated, it involves the use of the operators AND, OR, or NOT to specify subsets. For example, in searching a bibliography of books about cities, to specify Chicago AND Paris would locate all the citations that refer to both Chicago and Paris. To specify Chicago OR Paris would locate all citations that referred to either Chicago or Paris. A request for Paris AND NOT Chicago would find only those references to Paris that did not also refer to Chicago.

boot — Term derived from "pulling yourself up by your own bootstraps." It describes the process wherein the computer clears its memory, runs a self-test, and loads the operating system after it is either powered up (cold or hard boot) or reset (warm or soft boot). Instructions for booting are stored in each computer's ROM.

boot record — Track 0 on an IBM PC-compatible disk or the boot block on a Mac disk. This is the location on the disk that the ROM instructs to computer to read when the computer is booted.

bps — *bits per second*. The number of bits that are transferred in one second is used to rate the performance of asynchronous communications, typically a modem or a serial port. These speeds have continued to increase. The familiar speeds of ten years ago, 300 and 1200 bps, have been largely replaced by 9600 bps, 19,200 bps, and even 115,200 bps speeds. What these numbers mean in a practical sense is that, for a 9600 bps transmission, 9600 bits or 1200 bytes, each representing one character, will be transmitted from one device to another in just one second.

bridge — Device that enables two different local area networks to exchange data.

broadband — Analog communications method characterized by high transmission capacity (bandwidth). Its capacity allows it to be split into multiple communication channels. Operating over long distances at great speeds, it can transmit both voice and data communications.

buffer — Area of memory used to store information temporarily. These memory pools are particularly useful when different parts of the computer system (such as a printer and the CPU) operate at different speeds. Some software programs for PC-compatible computers require that a certain number of buffers be pre-defined when the computer is booted. This is done by the use of the BUFFERS= statement located in the CONFIG.SYS file.

bug — Programming error that makes a computer or program generate incorrect or unexpected results. The term derives from the story of an insect that made its way inside the early ENIAC computer and created such errors.

bulletin board system (BBS) — A computer system accessible by modem that usually is operated by and for a group of individuals with shared interests. Bulletin boards provide functions such as simple electronic mail and file upload, storage, and download capabilities. Bulletin boards devoted to all kinds of topics are available all over the country and the world. In the past, such systems used to be an excellent way to get public domain software or shareware. However, computer viruses sometimes are hidden in these bulletin boards and downloading from them should be done very carefully.

bus — The pathway that a computer uses to send signals from one part of the computer to another.

bus topology — Type of local area network configuration. In it, all nodes (computers, shared peripherals, and file servers) are connected to a single communications trunk line.

byte — *Eight bits.* One of the basic units of storage for computers. Typically, each character (letter, number or other) takes one byte to store. A kilobyte is 1024 bytes (2^{10}) and a megabyte is 1,048,576 bytes (2^{20}). In practical terms, one double-spaced page of text can be stored in about 1900 bytes; a 300-page manuscript will take 570,000 bytes.

C

cache, disk — Area of RAM used by the operating system to store the most recently called data and program segments assuming that they will be called again. As the disk cache is filled, the older code and data are replaced by the most recent. The use of a disk cache can improve the speed performance of disk-intensive programs.

cache, memory — Special section of RAM, designated to hold the most frequently used information. Controlled by a special cache controller chip, this memory increases the speed of a computer system because the microprocessor does not have to wait for the slower dynamic random-access memory (DRAM).

CADD — *Computer-Aided Drafting and Design.* The creation and design of any number of objects, from homes to cars to ancient pottery, using computers and specially crafted drawing and design programs. Many of these design programs had to be run on large mainframe or minicomputers because of their memory, speed, and storage requirements. With the appearance of the faster, more powerful microprocessors (Intel's 386 and 486 and Motorola's 68030), more CADD is being done on microcomputers.

CAI — *Computer-Assisted Instruction.* Software specifically designed for instructional purposes. The types of CAI programs available are wide ranging from simple drill and practice exercises to extensive hypermedia applications that integrate text with video and audio. Those who dismissed the possibilities of CAI based on the inflated claims of ten years ago might be surprised by the options and possibilities available today.

card — Electronic circuit board that fits into a computer's expansion slots and adds additional functions or resources to the computer. Also called an adapter or expansion board.

Cartesian coordinates — Reference system for two-dimensional graphics that locates any given point on an *x* and *y* grid. This is the system used in many mapping, graphics, and desktop publishing programs.

cartridge font — Cartridge designed for printers that provides fonts beyond the base fonts provided with the printer.

CD-ROM — Read-only storage device that uses compact disks. The optical technology allows large quantities of information to be stored on these disks. For this reason, this medium has started to be widely used to store large-scale collections of information.

CD-ROM disk drive — Device that allows a computer to access information from a CD-ROM.

CGA — Color Graphics Adapter. Bit-mapped graphics display adapter for PC-compatible computers that allows four colors to be displayed simultaneously at a resolution of 200 (horizontal) and 320 (vertical) pixels. A CGA adapter can connect to either a composite or RGB monitor.

chip — An integrated electronic circuit miniaturized on a small piece of silicon. The technology was introduced in the late 1950s that allowed semiconducting materials to duplicate the functions of transistors and other electronic components. Their size and the fact that these chips can be mass produced has made it possible to build computers that are ever smaller and less expensive. Different kinds of these chips serve as the microprocessor and the memory of microcomputers as well as a variety of other support functions, such as disk drives and video cards.

Chooser — Desktop Accessory for Macintosh that lets the user switch between devices available to the computer. In a stand-alone system with one printer, the Chooser might never be used. In a network environment it might be used to select printers, access a file server, or connect to the electronic mail system.

circuit board — Plastic board that has circuits manufactured into it.

CISC — *Complex Instruction Set Computer*. This common type of microprocessor recognizes many different instructions. Although this kind of chip has dominated personal computers, an increasing number of faster RISC (Reduced Instruction Set Computer) chips are being developed.

click(ing) — Action on a mouse or similar device that indicates the highlighted choice should be used. Depending on the application, a single click (pressing down on the button) or double click can trigger different responses from the computer.

clipboard — Temporary storage area in computer's memory. The area stores text or graphics that can be cut, copied, moved, or pasted to another location. Different programs refer to this as a buffer or glossary.

clock speed — Speed of microprocessor's internal clock measured in megahertz (MHz). The speed indicates how fast a computer processes CPU-based tasks. Early processors like the 8088 operated at 4.77 MHz; chip speeds of 33 MHz are not unusual today.

CMOS — *Complementary Metal-Oxide Semiconductor.* A chip that duplicates the functions of other chips but uses less electricity. For that reason, they are most often used in battery-powered laptop computers.

coaxial cable — Connecting cable with a high bandwidth used with broadband systems and fast baseband systems. It can carry more information than twisted pair (telephone wire) cable.

coding scheme — A method of organizing data into a format eaier for the computer to process. Usually included are a description of where the computer will find particular information and any numeric representations of category values (e.g., the field SEX can be found in column 5 of the input record and the valid codes are 0 [male] and 1 [female]).

COMMAND.COM — System file in DOS that contains the instructions the computer needs to run. This file must be present on the boot disk for DOS to run.

command-driven program — Program that requires user to enter commands to run. Many computer users feel that these programs are more difficult to use than menu-driven programs in which all commands appear on the screen. Other users feel that command-driven programs provide more user control.

communications protocols — Settings that two computers must have in common to communicate with each other. When using a microcomputer to communicate with a host computer, the communications program on the micro must be set to be consistent with that of the host. Most often these involve the baud rate, data bits, duplex, parity, stop bits, and, sometimes, handshaking.

communications software — Software application that lets one microcomputer access another, remote computer. Most communications programs allow one machine to communicate directly to another machine via modem and upload and download files over telephone lines or some other channel.

compact disk (CD) — An optical storage medium that currently stores about 650 megabytes of digitally encoded data. Most of these plastic disks currently provide read-only storage; these are referred to as CD-ROMs. Once information is placed on the disk it cannot be changed, nor can new information be written on the disk. Thus, these storage devices are most often used for large databases and collections that don't need to be changed. Erasable optical disks are expected to be one of the growth technologies of the 1990s.

compatibility — One of the major problems confronting the computer industry. Compatibility means the ability of software or peripherals to work equally well on different brands of computers. The term IBM PC-compatible means that programs, peripherals, and adapters work as well on the compatible computer as on an IBM-PC.

composite video — Standard video signal, established by the U.S. National Television Standards Committee (NTSC). Used by some computers and monitors, the standard is an analog video signal that mixes the colors of red, green, and blue to create colors on the screen.

compressed file — File created by a utility program that reduces the amount of storage space required for the file.

CompuServe — For-profit bulletin board system that has become one of America's largest on-line information services. Services provided range from weather reports, airline reservations, stock market quotations, and shopping to on-line conferences on a variety of topics.

CONFIG.SYS — Text file used by DOS and OS/2 to store configuration commands that will be loaded at boot time.

configuration file — A file created when installing an applications program that defines the options and peripherals that the program will use. This configuration file, for example, will contain information on the printers or the type of video display attached to the computer.

connectivity — The degree to which applications, computers, and peripherals fit into a networked environment.

connector — Terminator/connection device at the ends of a computer cable. Often these cables are referred to in gendered terms. Connectors that have protruding pins are known as male, connectors with receptacles for those pins are known as female.

context switching — In a multiple-loading operating system, activating one program to the foreground. Unlike in a true multitasking system, where several applications can run at once, in a multiple-loading system, the background application stops executing. Context switching allows for rapid switching between foreground and background applications.

control code — One of thirty-two ASCII codes reserved for hardware control purposes such as a beep or a printer page eject.

control panel — Utility menu used by Macintosh, Windows and OS/2 Presentation Manager to adjust system settings. These settings include such options as date and time, the desktop patterns and colors, and the size of the RAM cache.

control unit — Element of the CPU that receives instructions and directs the computer to accomplish them.

controller card — Adapter that connects disk drives (floppy or hard) with the computer's CPU and motherboard.

copy protection — Hidden instructions in software designed to prevent illegal copying or pirating.

courseware — Software developed for instructional purposes.

CP/M — *Control Program for Microprocessor*. This operating system was used for Intel 8080 and Zilog Z-80 microprocessors and is no longer widely used.

CPU — *Central Processing Unit*. The CPU functions as the computer's brain. It follows the instructions provided by the software and lets the hardware interact with the software and the user. The CPU consists of the ALU, the control unit, and the primary storage. The first two are contained on the microprocessor and the storage is linked to the microprocessor on either the motherboard or through the expansion bus.

crash — Any irregular ending of a computer program or session. Serious crashes can cause the computer to lock up and data to be lost.

cross-sectional data — Data collected at one point in time.

CRT — *Cathode Ray Tube*. Common type of computer monitor that uses a cathode to display the phosphorus on the screen.

cursor — Character visible on screen that indicates where the next character will appear.

cursor movement keys — Keys on keyboard that move the location of the cursor on the screen.

cylinder — A unit of storage on disk drives consisting of the tracks that occupy the same position. On a double disk drive, for example, a cylinder would be the same track number on both sides.

DA — Desk Accessory. A set of utility programs that are useful in everyday activities, providing things such as an on-screen calculator and a phone dialer. Used primarily by Macintosh computers.

D

daisy-chained — One method for linking computers and other devices. In a daisy chain, one device's output is linked to another device's input. One problem with daisy chaining is that if one device breaks or becomes disconnected, all other devices behind it on the chain will also stop working.

daisy-wheel printer — Impact printer that uses a daisy wheel to create type similar to that on a typewriter. The daisy wheel looks something like a bicycle wheel with letters located at the outer edge of the spokes.

database — Any set of related information organized in a way that permits data to be used for further analysis. In the most literal sense, a collection of note cards taken for a particular project can be considered to be a database. Most databases consist of discrete records corresponding to logical units such as people, books, or court cases.

database, fixed-field — A database system that requires each record to be structurally exactly the same as each other record. In such a database, each field is predefined with given characteristics such as type and length. For example, a database might be created to keep track of undergraduates in a class. That database might contain a NAME field that could store 25 characters; 5 numeric fields of 3 digits each to store the points awarded for two essays, a midterm, a final, and the total points; and a final two-character field, GRADE, in which the final grade was recorded. Each record (one for each student) would have the same structure of 42 characters and numbers (25 + 5 x 3 + 2) although the contents of each individual field would differ by student.

database, free-field — A database system that does not impose a rigid structure on each record. The most common of these databases used by historians are the text-oriented databases that include long descriptive fields or the note-taking database programs that permit the user to include as much or as little text as appropriate.

database, hierarchical — Database structured so that certain records "belong" to other records according to a structure that is imposed at the time the database is created. Hierarchical databases can be used in many of the same ways as relational database systems, but they are often less flexible, especially in changing the original hierarchy.

database management system — *(DBMS)*. Application software that permits the creation and modification of databases, the retrieval of information from a database, and the updating of information already stored in the system.

database management system, relational — Particular type of DBMS that allows information from multiple databases to be joined (related) on identifiers common to all databases. These database systems are more flexible than flat-file database systems that allow access to only one file at a time.

database, text-oriented — Database designed to be used with textual data. See also database, free-field.

data communications — Generally, the transfer of data over telephone or other wires.

data file — File created that contains the information created by a program. A data file is usually distinguished from a program file that executes an application.

data table — Database management term to describe the presentation of data on screen in a columnar fashion.

data type — In some applications, a description of the kind of data that will be stored in a field or variable. Common types include character (any letter or number that is always treated as text), numeric (digits and decimal points on which numeric calculations can be performed), and logical (true or false).

default — The action, setting, name, drive, or other function that will take over if no other instructions are provided.

delimiter — Some kind of symbol that indicates the end of one command or piece of information and the beginning of another. In written text, for example, a space serves as a delimiter between words.

demodulation — A telecommunications term that describes the process wherein the analog signal of the phone line is translated into the digital equivalent for the computer.

density — Measure of the number of bits that can be stored in a square inch of a device like a floppy disk.

desktop — On a computer using an operating system with a graphical user interface (like the Macintosh or an IBM PC-compatible running Microsoft Windows), a screen representation of an actual desktop, complete with folders.

desktop computer — A computer or workstation designed to fit on a desktop. Most microcomputers fit into this classification until the development of laptop and notebook computers.

device — Any piece of hardware that can receive and/or send data. Examples include a printer, monitor, and keyboard.

device driver — A supplemental software program that tells the operating system how to work with a particular device such as a printer or mouse.

dialog box — An on-screen box that gives or asks for information from a user. Dialog boxes are widely used in graphical user interfaces.

dial-up (access, lines) — Specially designated phone lines that permit remote users to connect to a host computer using a modem. Increasingly, libraries and other such organizations use dial-up lines to give users easier access to their on-line catalogs.

DIF file — *Data Interchange Format file.* A standard format used by the early spreadsheet program, Visicalc, that permitted data exchange between different programs.

digital — The representation of information by discrete objects (digits). In a digital computer, those digits are bits. These bits are used alone and in combination to accomplish all the tasks of the computer.

digitize — To convert an image into a digital or electronic representation of that image. This can be done using a specially designed digitizer or digitizing tablet that lets a user trace the outline of an object and translates the points traced into the electronic format. Scanners can also be used to digitize an image.

DIP switch — *Dual In-Line Package.* On/off switch connector used to select operating settings for the circuit board. Most DIP switches are now positioned on a panel for easy user access if they are used at all.

direct-connect modem — Modem that connects directly to the phone line through a modular jack. This type of modem has largely replaced the earlier acoustic modem that required the telephone headset to be placed in the modem.

directory — In DOS and OS/2, a listing of all the files stored on a disk or a subdirectory of the disk. On the Macintosh, the directory window displays the icons (or other presentation if requested) of all the files in a designated folder.

disk — Storage device for computers. See floppy disk, hard disk, and compact disk for a more detailed discussion of various types of disks.

disk drive — Secondary storage device that reads from and/or writes to a floppy diskette, a hard drive, or a CD-ROM.

distributed processing system — Computer system for multiple users wherein each user has a fully functional computer. These systems are usually designed to improve communications between the individual computers on the system and to share information and peripherals. Most microcomputer local area networks are distributed processing systems.

DOS — *Disk Operating System.* The operating system used by IBM-PC compatible microcomputers. On machines manufactured by IBM, the operating system is more precisely called PC-DOS. On compatibles, the system is known as MS-DOS after Microsoft, the company that developed it.

dot-matrix printer — Printer that creates letters by hitting a combination of pins on the ribbon, in effect filling in dots on a matrix. The appearance of the individual characters created by a dot-matrix printer depends on the number of pins (usually 9 or 24) used to create it.

double-density — Reference to the amount of information that can be stored on a floppy disk. The double refers to the fact that information is stored twice as densely as on the earliest single-density diskettes.

download — Process by which files are transferred from one computer to another computer or device. Downloading implies copying a file from the host computer to a local computer.

downloadable font — Printer font that must be copied from the computer's disk drive to the printer's RAM before it can be used. Downloadable fonts generally provide a wide range of styles and sizes but also require that the printer have large amounts of available RAM and often take time to download.

downward compatibility — Software or hardware that runs on or works with earlier models of equipment. An upgrade to a word-processing package that continues to run on the same equipment as did an earlier version would be downwardly compatible. If the newer version now required more memory or more hard disk storage, it would not be.

dpi — dots per inch. A measure of the resolution of both screens and printers. The higher the number of dots per inch, the better the resolution of the characters and graphics formed.

DRAM — Dynamic Random-Access Memory. Type of random-access memory chip that uses electrical charges to represent the contents of memory. The memory is called dynamic because when the electricity is turned off, the content of the memory is lost. The speed of these chips in refreshing memory is measured in nanoseconds (ns). It is important when adding or replacing DRAM chips that the speed of the chips is appropriate to the microprocessor.

draw(ing) packages, programs — Graphics software that allows users to draw graphics images freehand using a mouse or other input device. Most of these packages also include a variety of other tools that facilitate the creation of these images.

DTP — DeskTop Publishing. The use of a personal computer with appropriate applications software and printing devices to create typeset-quality text and graphics. The ability of these systems to merge graphics and text on a single page and to create camera-ready copy has made this one of the faster growing areas of personal computing.

duplex printing — Printing on both sides of a piece of paper.

Dvorak Keyboard — Alternate to the standard QWERTY keyboard. The keyboard was first designed for typewriters to minimize the number of times fingers need to leave the home row.

EARN — European Academic Research Network. A European wide area network that is fully integrated with BITNET for electronic mail communications.

E

EGA — Enhanced Graphics Adapter. Bit-mapped graphics adapter for IBM PC-compatibles that allows displays of up to sixteen colors and with a resolution of 640 pixels horizontally and 350 pixels vertically.

EISA — Extended Industry Standard Architecture. A 32-bit expansion bus created by a consortium of IBM PC-compatible computer makers. Unlike IBM's proprietary microchannel bus, this bus is compatible with earlier 16-bit peripherals.

electronic mail (e-mail) — Communications over electronic media. E-mail uses a store-and-forward technology that allows a user to send messages to another person or group of people whether they are currently logged on to the mail system or not. There are a variety of electronic mail networks, both public and private. Most colleges and universities now have their own mail systems and are linked to BITNET, Internet, NetNorth, or EARN. Private mail systems include CompuServe and MCIMail. To use any of these electronic mail systems, one must first secure an identification address where messages can be sent.

electronic publishing — Publishing in electronic rather than paper form — e.g., a manuscript created, edited, typeset, and produced, using publishing software, rather than traditional typewritten, typeset, and prepress production methods.

emulation — Action to make one device duplicate the function of another device. In communications software, for example, it is sometimes necessary to configure the personal computer to emulate a VT-100 or some other terminal to communicate with a mainframe.

encryption — A process that encodes data differently to prevent unauthorized users from using the file.

EPROM — *Erasable Programmable Read-Only Memory.* A ROM chip that can be reprogrammed to contain different instructions.

EPS — *Encapsulated PostScript File.* Such a file contains a graphics image created using the instructions of the PostScript page description language. These high resolution images can be transferred between different devices and different applications.

erasable optical (EO) disk drive — A secondary storage device that uses a laser and reflected light to read and write data. The erasable disk drives differ from CD-ROM and WORM drives in that they can be written on, erased and written on again.

escape code — A combination of the ESCape code and another ASCII character. These codes are sometimes used by printers to change printing styles and fonts.

ESDI — *Enhanced System Device Interface.* One of several standards for hard disk drives. Drives using ESDI transfer data at 10 megabits per second.

Ethernet — High-speed local area network standard developed by Xerox Corporation. Using a baseband single channel, it has a 10 megabit-per-second transfer rate and can include up to 1024 nodes on its network bus.

even parity — An error-checking technique used in asynchronous communications. One of the parameters that needs to be set before communicating with another computer.

event-driven programming — Program that will respond to actions initiated by the user, such as clicking a mouse.

expanded memory — Method of using memory beyond the 640k DOS-imposed limit. Software moves information back and forth into a 64k memory area so quickly that the computer appears to have more than the DOS limit.

expansion board — Circuit board designed to fit into the computer's expansion bus. These boards add to or expand the computer's functionality.

expansion bus — Part of computer's architecture that extends the actual data and address bus to accommodate a number of slots that can be filled with expansion boards.

expansion slot — Connector on a computer's expansion bus designed to hold additional adapter boards that enhance and expand the computer's functions and performance.

expert system — A type of artificial intelligence designed to capture an expert's knowledge on the topic and make it available to nonexperts. These systems contain both a knowledge base of information and a series of rules about using that information.

export — To write information from one applications program so it can be used by another program.

extended character set — A standard character set used by personal computers that includes foreign language, technical, and graphic symbols in addition to the 128 ASCII characters.

extension — Character string of 0-3 characters following the period in a DOS file name. These extenders often indicate the contents of the file. For example, dBASE data files default to an extension of .DBF, Lotus 1-2-3 files to .WK1, and Microsoft Word files to .DOC.

extended memory — Random-access memory (RAM) above 1M available for DOS and internal systems use on computers with 80286 and above microprocessors. DOS cannot utilize this additional memory fully because of its 640K base memory requirement. However, memory management programs can treat it as expanded memory, and operating systems like OS/2 can use its features more completely.

external hard drive — A hard drive attached externally to a microcomputer that usually comes with its own case, cables, and power supply. External floppy drives are also available.

external modem — A modem complete in its own case, meant to be attached to a computer via the serial port.

fax — Machine used to transmit and receive an image of a printed page via phone lines. Fax cards are now available for microcomputers that permit the computers to send and receive fax images (facsimiles).

field — A particular piece of information in a database. Associated with a particular name (often that describes the contents), the contents of a field vary with each record. In statistical software packages, fields are often called variables.

file — A collection of information stored together on a secondary storage device. Files are created by applications software and are controlled by the operating system.

file allocation table (FAT) — Hidden table on each floppy or hard disk that describes the locations of each file on the disk.

file attribute — Code stored with each file's directory entry that determines whether the file is visible or hidden, read-only or archive.

file compression utility — Utility program that compresses and uncompresses files to a more compact form that uses less disk space.

file conversion utility — Utility program that converts a file in one format to another file with a different format. Such utility programs are particularly useful for converting files created by one word processor into the format used by another word processor.

file fragmentation — Situation where files are not written on contiguous clusters on a disk's surface. Although this presents no threat to the data, it does mean that the disk drive's read/write head must jump around on the disk's surface to read the whole file, and that can slow access to the data. Utility programs to defragment files and thereby improve efficiency are widely available.

file locking — Option on local area networks that locks a file so it can be used by only one user at a time.

file name — Name given to a computer file. DOS files can have up to eight characters in the file name and three characters in the extender. DOS file names can not include spaces or several other special characters. Macintosh file names can be up to thirty-two characters long and can use all characters except a colon (:).

file recovery utility — Utility program used to restore an erased file. It is more likely that an erased file can be recovered if no other files have been created since the accidental erasure. If a file is accidentally erased, run the file recovery program immediately.

file server — A device on a local area network that holds the programs and data that can be used in common. Usually this file server is a computer; however, in some LANs, it can also be a proprietary device specially designed for that particular LAN.

file transfer utility — A utility program for the transfer of files between different computers. The most common of these programs transfer programs between Macintoshes and IBM PC-compatible computers and between desktop and laptop computers.

Finder — Utility distributed with the Macintosh computer to manage files and memory. The recently released System 7 includes a MultiFinder that permits multiple applications to run at the same time.

firmware — Software instructions stored in a computer's ROM or other circuitry, rather than on a disk.

flatbed scanner — An optical scanner that can translate a full-page image into a digitized representation in a file.

floppy disk — A removable type of secondary storage media that uses a flexible magnetic disk stored inside a plastic envelope (5½") or (3¼"). These disks store varying amounts of information, depending on their size, density, and whether information is written on one or both sides. Floppy disks have to be formatted or initialized for the particular machine and operating system on which they will be used.

Font/DA Mover — A Macintosh utility program used to install bit-mapped screen fonts in the System Folder. Once these fonts are installed, they are available for use through the font menu in the various applications.

font smoothing — Technique used by high-resolution laser printers to reduce potential distortions on text and graphics.

font, type — A set of letters, numbers, punctuation marks, and special characters in a given typeface, size, posture, and weight. Although most printers still come with just one typeface, they include multiple fonts because they can print several sizes plus bold (a different weight) and italic (a different posture). More sophisticated printers can print multiple typefaces as well, using either different fonts stored in the printer ROM, in font cartridges, or in downloadable fonts. Fonts are also important for the appearance of characters on the screen.

footer — Text that appears at the bottom of each page, such as a title or a folio (page number).

footprint — Amount of space used by a computer on a desk. Computer manufacturers continue to try to build computers with ever smaller footprints.

foreground — In a multitasking environment, the priority operating area. Applications running in the foreground are those that respond to keyboard input.

format — A term with multiple uses. For floppy and hard disks, to format (or initialize on the Macintosh) means to prepare the disk's surface so that it can be used to store and retrieve information. The format of a file, i.e., the way data are stored, is determined by the software used to create it; for example, an Excel file cannot be automatically read by WordPerfect. To format a document means to prepare it so it appears the way the user wants it to appear.

FORTRAN (FORmula TRANslator)— One of the earliest programming languages developed in the 1950s by IBM.

freenet — Term used to describe community-based wide area network free to all community users.

freeware — Software that has been made available for public use without charge, even though much of it is copyrighted.

front end — Program designed to make user access to another hardware or software system easier.

full duplex — A protocol for asynchronous communications that indicates that the communications link can send and receive information at the same time. Most communications software requires that the user indicate whether communications will be in full or half duplex.

function key — Programmable key (or key combination) that is used by applications programs to call various functions. On IBM PC-compatible machines, these are usually the keys identified with F1–F12. On the Macintosh, these F-keys are the number keys 0–9 used in combination with the Command and Shift keys. Certain programs like WordPerfect make heavy use of these keys in their operation.

G

gateway — A device that connects two local area networks or a local area network and a wide area network. Gateways have their own processors and memory and often are used to do any necessary conversions between the two networks.

gender changer — Special cable that extends an existing cable to change the gender of the connector to the other gender. In computer jargon, a male connector is one with pins. A female connector is one with receptacles for those pins.

gigabyte — 1,073,741,824, or 2^{30} bytes. Unit used to measure storage that is roughly equivalent to 1000 megabytes.

global — Everything. A global backup means backing up everything on a hard disk. A global search and replace means to search for all occurrences of a string in an entire document and to replace them. A global format in a spreadsheet means to change every cell to the indicated format.

glossary — An option in a word-processing package that allows the user to store commonly used text and insert it easily anywhere in the text.

grabber hand — An icon of a hand on the screen. By positioning the hand with a mouse, the indicated text or graphic can be moved elsewhere on the screen.

graphical user interface (GUI) — A user interface that combines the use of a mouse and bit-mapped graphics. Championed by the Macintosh and now used in Microsoft Windows and OS/2s Presentation Manager, this interface includes a variety of standard features including the desktop metaphor, on-screen display of fonts, and multiple on-screen windows.

graphics file format — Way in which graphics images are stored in a file for viewing on a screen or a printer. Different programs use different formats, and standardization is only beginning to appear.

graphics tablet — Input device that uses an electronic pen on a special tablet to record the pen's movement as a graphic image available to the computer.

gray scale — Series of shades of gray, beginning with white and ending with black, used in computer graphics.

gutter — Space between columns in a multiple-column page. This term is most widely used for typesetting and desktop publishing but also appears in many word-processing programs.

H

hacker — Depending on one's point of view, a computer fanatic or a sophisticated computer enthusiast. Hackers spend much time with computers and have contributed valuable information about how computers, software, and communications networks function.

half duplex — A protocol for asynchronous communications that indicates that the communications link can only use one signal at once. As a result, the two computers must take turns in transmitting. Most communications software requires that the user indicate whether communications will be in half or full duplex.

half-height drive — Disk drive that is only half as high as the original IBM PC disk drive.

handle — The small black squares that surround a selected object in an object-oriented graphics program.

handshaking — Protocols used in communications so the sending device knows when the receiving device is ready to receive. These are often included in the hardware, but sometimes they have to be provided by the software, especially when transmission is done via telephone wires.

hard copy — Printed copy. Often used as the ultimate backup for information stored on a disk.

hard disk — Secondary storage medium that uses several magnetically coated disks stored in a sealed unit with the read/write heads. These devices can store large amounts of information (hundreds of megabytes). Hard drives (internal and external) are usually connected using one of several standard controllers: ST506, RLL, ESCI, or SCSI. Differences between controllers and the hard disks themselves can lead to very different access speeds.

hardware — All the physical components that make up a computer system — its circuitry, disk drives, keyboard, video display, etc. Distinct from the software, the programs that tell the hardware what to do.

Hayes compatible modem — A modem that uses the Hayes instruction set to begin and end communications. This instruction set has become a default standard for telecommunications.

header — Text that appears at the top of each page, such as a title or a folio (page number).

hexadecimal — Base 16 number system that uses the digits: 0, 1, 2, 3, 4, 5, 6, 7, 8, 9, A, B, C, D, and E. Programmers often use hexadecimal numbers because they can be made to correspond so easily to the binary numbers used by the computer. However, most computer users should never have to worry about them.

hidden codes — Text formatting codes stored in a document but not visible on the screen. These codes permit word processors to display text the way it will look on the printer.

hidden file — File that resides on a disk but is not visible on the disk directory. These files are often used by operating systems or applications programs so they cannot be changed or accidentally deleted by users.

Hierarchical File System (HFS) — Macintosh disk storage system that permits files to be stored in folders within folders. HFS is similar to the directory/subdirectory option in DOS.

high density — Storage technique for disks. Floppy disks manufactured using this technique can store more than a megabyte of information (1.2 mb on a 5½" or 1.44 mb on a 3¼" disk).

high end — Top-of-the-line model of a computer line.

highlighting — Marking a block or range of text or cells for a subsequent operation such as formatting, moving, cutting, or copying. On the screen this highlighted text appears in reverse video or in a different color, depending on the display and software.

host computer — The computer that provides access to its software or data to other computers connected by networks or telecommunications.

HyperCard — Authoring language bundled with Macintosh that permits on-screen retrieval of text, graphics, and sound. Applications, known as stacks, are collections of cards of information that can be linked in a variety of ways.

hypermedia — An application that lets users add graphics, sound, video, and animation to a hypertext system. Some of the most innovative instructional packages and information retrieval systems being developed today use hypermedia.

hypertext — An application that allows the user to move through information using predefined associative links. Hypertext represents an attempt to let users approach information through non-lineal or nonsequential ways. At the most basic level, hypertext provides a way to do nonsequential reading and writing. In an ideal hypertext system, a user could highlight almost any word or concept in a document and jump directly into an explanation or other related text or, in a hypermedia system, visual or sound. In addition, the user would be able to create linkages rather than just relying on those provided by the programmer.

IBM 8514/A display adapter — Video adapter for PS/2 computers that uses the VGA circuitry on the board that produces a resolution of 1024 pixels horizontally and 768 vertically. **I**

IBM PC-compatible computer — Any personal computer that runs all the software and can incorporate all the hardware peripherals developed for the IBM PC, XT, or AT. These computers, often called clones, use Intel 8088, 8086, or 80286 microprocessors. Software compatibility continues at the 80386 and 80486 levels, but hardware is no longer fully compatible because of the diverging EISA and microchannel architectures.

icon — An on-screen symbol for a file, peripheral, or function. Icons are an integral part of any graphical user interface.

impact printer — Printer that creates a character on the paper by hitting an image of that character against an ink ribbon on to the paper.

import — Bring a file created by one applications program into another applications program.

incremental backup — Backup that only backs up files that have been created or modified since the last backup.

index — In word processing and special text-indexing programs, an index is just like an index for a book. It is a listing of the pages of a text on which key words and phrases, specified by the user, appear. In databases, an index is a special file of pointers that indicates the order of the records if sorted on a particular field or fields. Whereas sorting a database changes the actual physical order of the records, indexing allows the database to maintain its original order although all listings and searches appear to be in the indexed order.

index of dissimilarity — Statistical measure used to indicate the degree of geographic segregations between groups.

infection — State of a computer system with a virus. Like human infections, those of a computer are not always visible or readily apparent. To avoid having a computer infected, avoid pirated software and downloading from bulletin boards.

information retrieval — Finding information. In an electronic environment, the data (texts, numbers, images, etc.) are stored in a format and on a medium accessible to a computer. Specially designed applications software is used to locate particular information and make it available to the user.

inkjet printer — Printer that forms letters on a page by spraying ink from tiny jets. These printers are quiet and capable of producing high-quality output.

input — Information entered into the computer.

input device — Peripheral device that lets the user give input to the computer. The most common input devices are keyboards and mice. Others include scanners, trackballs, graphics tablets, and light pens.

installation program — A special program supplied with most applications that guides the user through the steps necessary to install the application on a computer. It is important to follow the instructions provided by these installation programs. Otherwise, it is possible that the applications program will either not run at all or run incorrectly.

instruction — A statement in machine language that the computer can process.

instruction set — All the instructions that a computer can perform.

integrated circuit — Also called IC or chip. Semiconductor circuit that contains thousands or millions of transistors and other electronic components. The microcomputer industry became possible as these integrated circuits became both smaller and more complex. This process of storing many components on a single silicon chip is known as large-scale integration (LSI). Those chips that have the highest number of electronic components are called VLSI chips — very large-scale integration.

integrated program — Applications software that contains several different types of programs, such as word processing, spreadsheet, and database management. The individual elements of such programs (like word processing) are usually not as powerful as their stand-alone equivalents, but their comprehensive nature makes them worthwhile investments for some users.

interactive processing — Type of computer processing now widely used in which user interacts directly with the computer's operations. Unlike batch processing in which users submitted a series of computer commands and waited for results, interactive processing lets the user initiate and observe virtually each step.

interactive videodisk — Technology that uses a computer to access video information stored on a videodisk. These interactive videodisks have become one of the more interesting tools in the expanding area of computer-assisted instruction.

interface — The connection between two objects. For computer users, the interface means the connection between the user and the machine. The graphical user interface is the graphically oriented operating system that is supposed to make it easier for the user to interact with the computer. Interface can also refer to the connection between two hardware devices.

interleaved memory — RAM that has been divided into two banks or pages so the microprocessor can access information in one bank while the other is being refreshed. This speeds the computer's access to the contents of memory.

internal hard disk — Hard disk built to fit inside the computer's case and take its power from the computer's power supply.

internal modem — A modem designed to fit inside a computer in one of the expansion slots.

Internet — Global set of wide area networks running the Internet Protocol (IP). These interconnected networks share a common address space and standard communications protocol (TCP/IP). This is the backbone network used by many other network systems.

I/O — Input/Output. The part of the computer's architecture that controls how data and instructions enter and leave the CPU.

J *join* — Linking records in two databases that are related to each other. Information kept in a registrar's office can serve as an example of this joining. Envision a database in which basic information is kept on each student, including an ID number and the address to which grades are to be mailed. In another database are the grades for all students enrolled in a given semester. Each record in that database also includes a student's ID number. The database management system used can join all the student's grade records with the record containing the mailing address because each contains the ID number that is used to relate the two databases.

joystick — Input device used by many computer games. A joystick uses a rotating lever that moves the cursor on the screen according to the direction the lever is moved.

justification — The alignment of text on the left, right, or both margins. When text is aligned on both margins, it is called full justification.

K *Kermit* — Rumored to be named after a famous frog, an asynchronous communications protocol used for transmitting files over phone lines. Columbia University developed a communications package based on this protocol and placed it in the public domain. Many academic institutions use Kermit for file transfers because it runs on mainframe computers as well.

kerning — Reducing space between letters to present a better visual image. An option available in most desktop publishing and some word-processing packages.

keyboard — Most common of the microcomputer input devices.

keyboard buffer — Memory area that allows the user to continue typing on the keyboard even if the computer is doing something else and not responding to the keyboard. When the buffer is full, the computer will beep.

key word — In programming, a word that causes the computer to take some action. In text-oriented databases, a user-defined word or phrase on which the computer can sort, retrieve, or otherwise manipulate.

kilobyte (K, k) — 1024 or 2^{10} bytes. A measure used for both a computer's internal memory and its storage devices.

knowledge base — The part of an expert system that represents an expert's knowledge.

knowledge domain — An artificial intelligence term for an area of expertise.

KWIC — Key Word In Context. A special type of key word searching that indicates the context in which it is used as well as the word itself.

LAN — Local Area Network. Any number of computers and peripherals linked by cables so they can share data, software, peripherals, and other resources. These LANs vary widely in size, complexity, and options. Some include three devices; others can be campuswide. Smallers LANs can be linked with each other via bridges and gateways. The basic components of each LAN include the cables, a network interface card that handles most of the networking tasks for the individual computers, personal computers, a file server, and appropriate peripherals, such as printers. These networks take one of four forms: bus, daisy chain, ring, and star — configurations that closely describe their physical layout. The transmission speed of these networks is largely determined by whether they use broadband or baseband technology in their cabling.

landscape orientation — Page orientation on a PC that allows the printer to print the image or text so the longer side of the page is horizontal instead of the typical (portrait) orientation where the image or text is printed so the shorter side is horizontal.

laptop computer — Lightweight (generally under twelve pounds), battery-powered computer. These computers, generally seen as a great advance in transportability over the heavier, luggable computers, are being rapidly challenged by the notebook computer, an even lighter, more portable model.

laser printer — Printer that uses a technology similar to that of photocopying machines to generate high-resolution text and images.

letter-quality printer — Printer designed to emulate the output of a high-quality typewriter. These printers produce high-quality text output but cannot produce high-quality graphics.

library — Collection of computer programs that are available for use within another program. For example, Microsoft Word makes access to its spelling checker and thesaurus available through its library option.

light pen — Light-sensitive stylus used with a special screen or graphics tablet to input information to the computer.

link — A connection between files or data. In linked files, a change in one is reflected in the other. In hypermedia, a connection established between one item and another, related item, such as a verbal description and a map, or a word and a photo.

liquid crystal display (LCD) — Display that requires very little energy and is widely used in laptop and notebook computers. The display uses crystal molecules that, when electrically charged, direct light to a screen to produce a dark area. These screens tend not to be bright enough to use comfortably for long periods of time, so many manufacturers have added back lighting to make the screen more readable in exchange for reducing the time the computer can run on batteries.

list servers — Method for broadcasting messages using electronic mail. Individuals subscribe to a list and their mail addresses are appended to a list of all subscribers. When a message is sent to the list, it is then forwarded to all members of the list.

load — Copy program or data from a secondary storage device, such as a floppy disk, into the computer's RAM, so it can be used.

local area network (LAN) — See LAN.

log off — Exiting from a computer system.

log on — Process by which a user gains access to a computer system. For most personal computer users, this log on procedure is most common for gaining access to a host computer and often involves an identifier and password.

longitudinal data — Data that contains a time element. Census information on a family that shows what the family's structure was in 1900 and 1910 is cross-sectional, that is, it shows a picture of the family at two distinct periods of time. A family bible that provides the information on the composition of the family as it changes is longitudinal.

M

machine language — Language used by the CPU. Ultimately all programs have to be translated into machine language before the computer can act on their instructions. All statements in machine language are symbolized by 0s and 1s to correspond to the electronic states used by the computer.

machine-readable — Image or text stored in a format that can be read by a computer.

Macintosh, Mac — Apple Computer's line of personal computers introduced in 1984. The Macintosh line was distinguished from earlier personal computers by its graphical user interface and brought many personal computer users into their first contact with mice and icons. The Macintosh line uses Motorola's 68000 series chip. Newer versions of the Macintosh were introduced in 1986 (Mac Plus), 1987

(Mac SE and Mac II). The Macintosh II represented a significant departure from other Macintoshes, not only in its use of the 68020 and 68030, but also in its open architecture.

macros — A named series of frequently used keystrokes, commands, or instructions that are stored to be called up later to accomplish a particular task. Macros are widely used to eliminate repetitious tasks or for automating certain procedures. Some applications programs include macro building options. Utility programs that work in conjunction with other applications permit users to build macros for those applications that do not.

magnetic disk — Random-access secondary-storage device widely used with personal computers. Disks have a magnetic coating that can store information.

mailbox — Storage location in an electronic mail system where messages are kept for a particular mail address until the person associated with that address reads them.

mainframe — Computer designed to support multiple users and meet large-scale computing needs. The distinction between mainframes and minis has become increasingly blurred. Generally a mainframe is considered to be the computer that provides computing for an entire organization, like a university. A mini provides the computing for a smaller unit, like a department.

MARC — *Machine-Readable Catalog.* A database standard developed to store archival catalogs on the computer. This has become the preferred format for these collections and has provided a means for creating a common catalog for archival and other non-book collections.

MCGA — *MultiColor Graphics Array.* Video display adapter developed by IBM for its PS/2 computers. It added sixty-four shades of gray to the older CGA standard and provided a 16-color 640 horizontal pixel by 350 vertical pixel resolution.

mean time between failures (MTBF) — Measure of the failure rate of equipment; the average length of time between when a particular piece of equipment is manufactured and the first time it fails.

Megabyte (M, Mb,) — Memory measure equivalent to 1,048,576, or 2^{20} bytes.

megaflop — One million floating point operations per second. A measure of the processing capabilities of workstations, minis, and mainframes.

megahertz (MHz) — One million electrical vibrations or cycles per second. A measure of the clock speeds of computers. The early 4.77 MHz speed of the 8088-based computers has climbed to speeds of 33 MHz.

memory — Primary storage area for computers, usually the RAM. This memory is differentiated from the secondary storage on devices like hard drives.

memory management software — Utility program designed to let DOS computers use the memory above 640k limit. These programs allow users to define and utilize expanded, extended, and virtual memory.

memory resident program — Program designed to reside in the computer's RAM while the computer is on so that it can be immediately accessed. These programs are also known as TSR (terminate and stay resident) programs.

menu — On-screen display that provides the user with a list of the options available at that time.

menu-driven program — Program designed so that all commands are issued through a menu. Menu-driven programs are generally considered to be easier to use than command-driven programs.

microchannel bus — Proprietary 32-bit bus architecture developed by IBM for its PS/2 line of microcomputers. This bus is not compatible with the earlier 16-bit bus design of the IBM AT.

microcomputer — A computer that has at its heart a microprocessor that contains both the ALU and control unit on one chip. Microcomputers are also usually seen as single-user machines; however, as they become more powerful, they can be used in centralized and distributed systems as well as in a stand-alone environment.

microprocessor — An integrated circuit containing the arithmetic/logic and control units of the central processing unit (CPU).

MIDI — *Musical Instrument Digital Interface.* Communications protocol that transfers data between computers and musical synthesizers. This particular combination allows musicians to play something on the keyboard and have it immediately changed to musical notation on the computer. The computer can then be used to change virtually all aspects of the digitized sound.

MIDI port — Port that permits a microcomputer to connect directly to a musical synthesizer.

minicomputer — A computer designed for smaller multiuser environments. Most minis are less powerful than mainframes and more powerful than micros.

MIPS — *Million Instructions Per Second.* A measure of the speed at which a computer executes instructions.

modem — *MOdulator/DEModulator.* A device used to change the digital signals produced by a computer to the analog signals used by the telephone lines and back again to the digital signals required by the receiving computer.

monitor — Another term for a video display unit (VDU) or cathode ray tube (CRT) attached to a computer that displays information passed from user to computer and vice versa.

monochrome display adapter — Single color display adapter for IBM PC-compatible computers. It displays text only with a resolution of 720 pixels by 350 pixels.

monochrome monitor — Monitor that displays only one color against either a black or white background.

motherboard — Printed circuit board that contains the central processing unit (CPU), support chips, random-access memory (RAM), and bus expansion slots.

mouse — Hand-held input device designed to be moved on a table top. Movements by the mouse generate signals that move a pointer on the screen. By pushing a mouse button (clicking) when the pointer highlights a menu option, the user can execute that option. Mice can be mechanical or optical and can be connected to a computer using a mouse port already on the computer, via the serial port, or by installing an expansion card that has the appropriate mouse connector. Mice have more than one button option.

MS-DOS — *Microsoft-DOS.* Operating system developed by Microsoft. IBM markets the version for its computers as PC-DOS; the version sold for compatibles is called MS-DOS. The two systems are virtually interchangeable.

ms (millisecond) — $\frac{1}{1000}$ of a second. Measure used to indicate the speed of devices like disk drives. A hard drive with a rating of 32 ms takes less time (and is therefore faster) than a disk that takes 90 ms to retrieve information from the disk's surface.

MultiFinder — Apple utility program that allows the Macintosh to run more than one program at a time. This is accomplished by context switching in a multiple-loading system.

multiple-loading operating system — An operating system that allows the user to load multiple programs into the computer's memory. Because only one program can be active at a time, this is not a true multitasking system.

multiplexing — Transmission of multiple messages over the same communications channel simultaneously. This ability is important in local area networks because it allows more than one computer to use the network at the same time.

multisynch monitor — Color display that adjusts to different frequencies so it can work with many different display adapters.

multitasking — Running multiple applications at one time on a computer. When multiple programs are running, the foreground task responds to input devices (keyboard, mouse, etc.) while the other applications continue to run in the background areas. Most newer operating systems now allow multiprocessing.

multiuser system — Computer that allows multiple users to share its programs and data simultaneously.

N

natural language processing — Branch of artificial intelligence that uses the computer to process language. Perhaps the most famous early attempt at natural language processing, although far from the most sophisticated, was ELIZA, the computer therapist.

near-letter-quality (NLQ) printer — Dot-matrix printer that uses a special near-letter-quality mode to print characters that approximate those of a letter-quality printer.

NetNorth — Canadian wide area network with the same functions as and fully integrated with BITNET.

network — Multiple computers connected by wires of cables. These networks can be for small areas (local area network) or span long distances (wide area network).

network interface card — Adapter that allows a personal computer to connect to a network cable. These adapters allow communications to take place at much higher speeds than would be possible through the serial port.

network operating system — System software for a LAN. These operating systems optimize network performance.

network topology — The physical layout of a network. Most networks are organized on a bus, daisy chain, star, or ring topology.

NeXT — Unix-based workstation initially designed for university use by Steve Jobs, one of the original founders of Apple Computer. Included in the initial model were an erasable optical disk drive, high fidelity sound, a graphical user interface, a PostScript display screen, and high-resolution printer.

node — Point on a LAN, usually a computer or a peripheral, that can send, receive, or forward a message.

notebook computer — Portable computer weighing about six pounds, capable of running various applications, such as word-processing, spreadsheet, and some database and graphics programs.

NSFNET — Wide-area network sponsored by the Office of Advanced Scientific Computing at the National Science Foundation.

ns (nanosecond) — one-billionth of a second. Speeds for computer memory are often recorded in nanoseconds. A memory chip rated at 80 ns means that information stored in that chip's memory can be retrieved in eighty nanoseconds.

NuBUS — Expansion bus of the Macintosh II computer.

null modem cable — Serial cable that has been specially configured to let two computers connect directly without the use of a modem or other intermediary device.

numeric coprocessor — Chip that performs mathematical computations many times faster than the microprocessor that it supports. These higher speeds are achieved by using 80-bit units to process information.

O

object-oriented graphics — Also known as vector graphics, images composed of objects such as lines and circles. Because objects are stored as mathematical formulas, it is easier to manipulate the size of these images without distortions than it is with comparable bit-mapped images.

OCLC — *Online Computer Library Center*. Massive bibliographic database that aims at providing a complete guide to the location of all book and nonbook holdings in libraries in the United States. This database is available on-line to libraries and certain other users.

odd parity — Error-checking protocol in asynchronous communications. A simple design, it counts the number of 1 bits in a byte. If the number is odd, the parity bit is set to 1; if even, to 0.

on-line — In communications, one computer connected to another computer. With printers, connected to the computer and able to receive information from it.

open architecture — Computer design that opens the computer itself through an expansion bus and the public availability of system specifications. The original IBM PC had an open architecture that helped to create a large number of clones and a booming peripheral industry. The original Macintosh had a closed architecture, i.e., the box was sealed and any add-ons had to be attached to the outside of the computer. The Macintosh II has an open architecture.

open bus system — Computer design that contains an expansion bus that accepts a variety of adapters.

Open System Interconnection (OSI) reference model — International standard for local area networks developed by the ISO (International Standards Organization) and IEEE (Institute of Electrical and Electronic Engineers).

operating system — Master control program that manages the computer's internal functions. The operating system must be loaded for the computer to run. Applications programs can only run with the help of the operating system. The most popular microcomputer operating systems are DOS, OS/2, and the Macintosh System. Unix is the operating system of choice on most workstations.

Operating System/2 (OS/2) — Multitasking operating system for IBM PC-compatible computers. OS/2 has gained acceptance slowly despite the fact that it overcomes the 640k barrier, takes full advantage of the protected mode of the Intel microprocessors to allow multitasking, and allows dynamic interchange of data between applications.

optical character recognition — Process by which a machine reads printed or typed text. Using images of characters available to the software, it matches each character scanned to images of characters recognized by the program and stores the ASCII code for the matched character in a file.

optical disk — Medium for secondary storage that uses a laser beam to read the presence or absence of tiny pits on the disk's surface. Because they are able to hold so much data, these disks promise to be one of the key storage media of the next decade.

orphan — Situation where the first line of a paragraph appears on one page while the rest of the paragraph appears on the next page. Word-processing and page layout programs generally provide user control over this problem and that of widows.

outline font — Font for screen or printer that uses a mathematical formula for producing each character. These outline fonts are considered superior to bit-mapped fonts because they are less susceptible to distortions, and one font can be scaled in virtually all point sizes instead of having to have a distinct font for each size.

output — The result of the computer's operations displayed on either the printer or screen.

P

page description language (PDL) — Programming language that describes printer output in terms of device-independent commands. To use these PDL commands, the printer has to have its own CPU and RAM. PostScript is one such PDL; TeX is another.

page layout program — Desktop publishing application program that can combine text and graphics, placing them precisely on the page in the form, size, and shape desired.

paint program — Application program that allows user to "paint" the screen by turning pixels on a bit-mapped screen on and off.

palette — Display of colors and patterns available in graphics applications.

parallel port — Port for synchronous communications. This port is used to connect devices like printers to the computer. Parallel communications are faster than serial communications because the eight bits in a byte are sent in parallel (i.e., at once over eight wires) instead of serially (i.e., sequentially, one at a time over one wire). Because of the problem of crosstalk (interference from one wire to another), parallel communications are only effective over short distances.

parallel processing — Another term for multitasking.

parameter RAM — In a Macintosh, battery-powered memory used to store configuration information when the power is off.

parity bit — An extra bit used to double check the contents of data as it is transmitted. This process, known as parity checking, is used primarily in asynchronous communications and for memory. If an error is discovered, the computer will advise that a parity error has been found.

park — Position a hard drive's read/write head to keep it from damage when it is moved.

path — The combination of directories and subdirectory (or folder) that a program will follow to find its data or program files. Paths may be specified in the file name (e.g., HARDDRIVE:FOX-BASE:ACTH) or, in the DOS environment, with the use of the PATH statement that informs the operating system which subdirectories it should look in for files (eg., PATH=C:\;C:\DOS;C:\WORD;C:\FOXPLUS;C:\QPRO) if they are not in the current directory.

PC-DOS — Special version of MS-DOS marketed by IBM with its personal computers.

peripheral — Device connected to and driven by a computer and physically distinct from the CPU. Printer, modems, and monitors are among the most common peripherals.

personal computers — Initially a computer designed to be small, independent, and able to perform a number of applications. With its peripherals, a personal computer could free individuals from mainframe computing and still accomplish their basic computing needs. As personal computers increase in computing power and become integrated into local and wide area networks, the definition of what a personal computer is and what personal computing involves becomes much broader. It is important to keep in mind that virtually all personal computers today are more powerful than the earliest computers like the ENIAC.

personal information manager (PIM) — Type of database management program designed to help an individual organize personal tasks and information. Most include such options as note taking, address or phone book, and appointment calendar.

pitch — Measure of the number of characters in a line of non-proportional type, the kind used by typewriters, letter-quality printers, and most dot-matrix printers. The most familiar pitches are elite (twelve characters per inch) and pica (ten characters per inch).

pixel — Picture element. The smallest unit that can be displayed on screen.

plasma display — Type of display used with high-end laptop computers. Images are created by energizing ionized gas stored between two panels.

platform independence — Ability of a local area network to connect computers from different manufacturers.

plotter — Output device that creates images and text by moving pens over the surface of the paper. Commands from the computer tell the plotter which pen to use, where to position it, and which direction to move with the pen.

point — Unit of measure in typography widely used in laser printers. One point equals 1/72 of an inch.

pointer — On-screen symbol that shows the current position of the pointing device—mouse, trackball, or light pen. In a database or programming language, a pointer is a key that points to a particular record or piece of information.

port — Plug on the computer that sends or receives electronic signals.

portable computer — Computer designed to be moved. Portable computers have continued to get smaller and smaller. Different categories of portable computers have emerged based on their size and weight. The first were known as luggables. These were replaced by laptops, which are being replaced by notebooks, and palmtops are now on the horizon.

portrait orientation — Default orientation for a printed page. Characters are printed horizontally along the shorter (usually 8½") width of the paper.

post — To send a notice to an electronic bulletin board. Directly comparable to pinning a notice on an actual bulletin board.

postmaster — Person with the responsibility of maintaining an electronic mail system. The postmaster makes sure the system functions, answers questions on its use, and generally keeps it running.

PostScript — Adobe Systems' page description language. PostScript is full programming language; however, most users need to know nothing about the language. Applications programs that contain PostScript drivers take care of generating the necessary programming commands that drive the output device. PostScript itself is device-independent, because printers contain PostScript interpreters that read the commands and fit them to the maximum capacity of the printer.

powerful — Term used to describe the capabilities of a computer or a piece of software. For software, power is usually equated with its number of functions and its capabilities. Hardware power is measured in terms of speed and computing instructions.

power supply — Electrical component in computer that takes the standard AC current and changes it to the DC current necessary for the computer.

presentation graphics — Charts, graphs, and other such enhanced images produced by computers that are used in presentations.

Presentation Manager — Graphical user interface and applications programming interface jointly developed by Microsoft and IBM for use with OS/2.

primary storage — The main memory of the computer. Unlike secondary storage on devices like disk drives, this memory is directly available to the computer's CPU.

printer driver — File containing all the instructions an applications program needs to print to a particular printer. In DOS machines, applications programs have to provide their own printer drivers. Under Windows and in the Macintosh environment, the printer drivers are provided by the system.

print spooler — Utility that lets the computer print files in the background while another program runs in the foreground. Multiple files can wait to be printed in the print queue.

program — Commands written in a computer programming language that tells the computer what to do.

programmable read-only memory (PROM) — Chip programmed at the factory that contains read-only memory (ROM).

programming language — Language such as FORTRAN, COBOL, BASIC, or PROLOG that, through the use of interpreters, translators, and compilers, provides instructions for the computer to implement.

prompt — Signal, usually in the form of a symbol or text, that indicates that the computer is ready to receive information from the user.

proportional spacing — Method of spacing text based on the width of a character. On a typewriter, each letter takes up the same space as any other letter; on a proportional-spacing printer, for example, an i will be allocated less space than an m.

protected mode — Operating mode in Intel's 80286 and newer microprocessors that protects the memory space used by one program from another program running at the same time.

public domain software — Software that is not copyrighted and can be distributed without permission or paying a fee. Despite the actions of many people, all software is not public domain software.

pull-down menu — A command menu that appears after clicking on or otherwise choosing the menu's name.

punch cards — Early input medium for computers, also known as Hollerith cards or IBM cards. Each paper card had eighty columns and twelve rows. The location of the hole (or holes) punched in the rows and columns represented a character or number to the computer. These cards were punched using a keypunch machine.

Q

query — A search in a database that indicates the kind of data that should be retrieved. Although database systems are designed to make querying easy, the user can develop special skills in searching that help insure that the information retrieved is what is wanted. This is especially true with the large, public databases such as Social Science or Humanities Index.

queue — A waiting line. The most common queue for microcomputers is the print queue — the documents or files waiting to be printed.

QWERTY — The six letters in the upper left row of letters on a standard typewriter and computer keyboard. These letters are used to describe this standard keyboard.

R

radio button — Round option button used in the dialog boxes in a graphical user interface. Radio buttons indicate that only one can be chosen.

RAM — *Random-Access Memory.* This memory is volatile because information can only be stored there temporarily. All the contents of RAM disappear when the computer is turned off.

RAM cache — A portion of the random-access memory that is used as a buffer between the CPU and disk drives to speed processing.

RAM disk — Portion of the random-access memory treated as if it were a disk drive. Applications and/or data are copied into the RAM drive so they can be accessed more quickly. The advantage of this is that it makes processing much faster, especially in applications that are highly disk dependent. The RAM disk and its contents have to be recreated each time the computer is turned off.

random-access — Means of retrieving information that allows the system to go directly to the information instead of having to proceed sequentially through everything in front of it. In effect, this is the difference between looking for a particular song on a record and a tape. On the record, you can position the needle at the appropriate location. With a tape, you have to fast-forward until you reach the place you want.

read/write head — Magnetic device that writes information to and reads it from the surface of a hard or floppy disk drive. The head moves back and forth across the surface of the disk to find the requested information.

record — One unit in a database and the collection of fields pertaining to it. In a bibliographic database, each book would be a record. In a database that contained individual manuscript census information, each person would be a record. A statistics software package would refer to the unit as a case.

refresh — To repeat. Both the computer's display and RAM must be refreshed constantly to keep the image and the information from being lost.

relational — See database management system, relational.

relational operator — Operators used to test relationships between values on the computer. These include = (equal to), < (less than), > (greater than), <> (not equal), <= (less than or equal to) and > = (greater than or equal to).

removable storage media — A secondary storage device that permits the storage medium (a magnetic disk, a Bernoulli cartridge, a CD-ROM) to be removed.

resolution — Measurement of the sharpness of an image, usually on a screen or printer. Resolution is often given in terms of dots per inch.

retrieval — Operation that allows user to find, display, or otherwise use information. The term is generally associated with databases, but can apply to most applications programs.

reverse video — Method of highlighting a block of text on the screen. If the text is normally displayed as black on white, in reverse video it would be displayed as white on black.

RGB monitor — Color monitor that accepts separate images for red, green and blue. This type of monitor was most widely used with the color graphics adapter.

ring network — A local area network in which the computers and peripherals are connected on a closed loop or ring. Each node on the network has a unique address and receives only the messages addressed to it.

RISC — *Reduced Instruction Set Computer.* A computer designed to operate using a minimal set of instructions. Fewer instructions permit the computer to run faster. These machines are often designed for particular types of computing.

RLIN — *Research Libraries Information Network.* Developed by the Research Libraries Group, this network is available to researchers throughout the United States through Internet. It contains bibliographic databases of holdings as well as such nonbibliographic databases as the Medieval and Early Modern Data Bank. It is also developing a database with the MLA on research in progress by members of that organization.

RLL — *Run Length Limited* recording. Method used by some hard disk drives to store and access information. This technique increases the amount of information that can be stored on a drive.

ROM — *Read-Only Memory.* Contents of the ROM are permanently burned into the chip and remain there whether the computer is on or off. Instructions stored in the ROM are known as firmware.

root directory — The main directory of a DOS disk created at the time the disk is formatted. All other directories created are subdirectories of the root directory.

RS-232 — One EIA (Electronic Industries Association) standard for asynchronous transmission of data. An updated version of this standard, the RS-232c, is used on most IBM PC-compatibles.

RS-422 — Another EIA standard for asynchronous transmission of data used on Macintosh computers.

S

satellite — A terminal or workstation linked to a host computer.

scanner — A peripheral that scans an image and translates the image into a digitized representation of it. This file can then be edited or merged into another program. With the use of an optical character recognition program, scanners can also read documents and translate them into text files. Flat-bed scanners (that resemble photocopying machines) scan full-page images. Hand-held scanners can usually scan only a 4-5 inch-wide section of a page at once; however, software accompanying those scanners can join the two halves of the page into a whole.

scientific notation — A method of presenting a number that has a -E or +E in it. The number following the E indicates the number of places the decimal point should be moved. The - or + indicates whether it should be moved to the left or right. The number 6.12345+E4 is equivalent to 61,234.5. The number 6.12345-E4 is equivalent to .000612345.

scrapbook — Macintosh desk accessory that stores data for future use.

screen font — Bit-mapped font that looks as much as possible like its equivalent printer font.

screen-saver utility — Utility that blanks the screen when the computer has not been used for a set period of time. As soon as a key is pressed, the screen is restored. Such a utility is particularly useful with a phosphorous screen, which can burn a permanent shadow onto the screen, but helps prolong the sharpness and life of all screens.

scroll bar/scroll box — Elements of a graphical user interface screen that allows the user to scroll through a document either horizontally or vertically.

SCSI — *Small Computer System Interface*. A standard interface for high-speed parallel-data transmission used to connect devices like disk drives and printers.

search — A command in an application that locates a particular character, string of characters, record, or entry. Commonly used in word-processing and database programs to facilitate text corrections or to find specific information.

sector — A segment of one of the tracks on the surface of a disk drive. When a disk is formatted or initialized, sectors are assigned.

seek time — Length of time it takes the read/write head to reach the desired location on the disk.

sequential access — Method of retrieval information that requires the computer to move sequentially through the data until it finds the requested information. This method is generally slower in accessing the information.

serial port — Port that permits asynchronous information to move in and out of the computer. It is called a serial port because the data moves serially, one bit at a time. Although slower than parallel communications, asynchronous communications can be accomplished over long distances without risk of data interference.

server — Computer on a local area network that provides services for the other computers and peripherals on the network.

shareware — Copyrighted software packages that are made available at a limited cost. Sometimes shareware is distributed on bulletin boards and other public arenas. In those instances, the user is expected to send the cost of the product to the developer to register ownership.

shell — Utility program used to provide a simpler interface between the user and an operating system or applications program.

SIG — *Special Interest Group.* These are individuals with common interests who use a particular bulletin board or belong to a particular organization. SIGs are excellent ways to find out detailed information and tricks for using particular pieces of hardware and software.

SIMM — *Single In-Line Memory Module.* Plug-in memory modules that are used to add memory to newer computers. These modules are significantly easier to install than the individual chips that were used in earlier personal computers.

simulation — Technique that uses the computer to model situations and objects. Historical demographers and economic historians have used simulations to gain useful insights into the past. Graphic image simulations can recreate past objects and landscapes from extant historical artifacts.

site license — Agreement between a software manufacturer and an organization that makes multiple copies of the software available for use inside the organization at reduced costs. Many colleges and universities arrange these site licenses to lower costs. Before buying an expensive piece of software, particularly one that others might want to use, one should check to see whether an institutional site license exists.

software — Instructions provided to the computer that are not part of its physical components. Applications packages, operating systems, and utility programs are all part of the computer's software.

software package — Commercially marketed and copyrighted applications programs.

software piracy — Any unauthorized or illegal duplication or distribution of copyrighted software. A piece of software is as protected by copyright law as a book.

speech synthesizer — Device that lets a computer produce an audio output that can imitate human speech. The best quality synthesizers replicate speech quite adequately.

spreadsheet programs — The software that convinced businesses to join the microcomputer revolution. A spreadsheet is laid out in rows and columns to emulate an accounting worksheet. Its cells (the intersection of a row and column) can contain numbers, labels (text) or formulas. The speed and ease of use of these applications, along with their ability to create graphic representations of the data, made them extremely powerful.

stack — File containing one or more cards created in HyperCard.

stand-alone computer — A computer that is not joined to any other computer by a network or other means. Complete with the software and peripherals, a stand-alone computer provides the computing power necessary for one person.

star network — Type of network typology where all nodes are linked to a central computer or equivalent processor. The name derives from the fact that the cables that link the individual nodes to the central computer give the physical configuration of a star.

start bit — A bit used in serial communications that indicates that it should begin reading a byte of data.

state-of-the-art — The latest, most powerful, most sophisticated piece of computer hardware or software. What no individual computer user will ever really own because a new state of the art will have emerged before the previous one reaches the stores. When buying a computer or piece of software, do not worry about whether it is state-of-the-art. Worry instead whether it will meet your current needs and those that you project for the next five years.

static random-access memory — RAM chip that does not need to be constantly refreshed. The ability to retain the information stored there means that it is faster than dynamic random-access memory (DRAM) and is more appropriate for the higher speed microprocessors.

statistical software — Applications program designed to analyze data statistically. Many of the statistics packages that first drew historians to mainframe computers have been migrated down to microcomputers. In the process, they have been made easier to use and have incorporated many of the advantages of microcomputers such as graphics.

stop bit — Bit signal used in asynchronous communications to indicate that a byte has been transmitted.

string — Any number of alphanumeric characters.

style sheet — Predefined text formatting instructions used by many word processors and page layout programs. Used intelligently, these style sheets can be a very effective way of formatting and reformatting a document, even at the level of footnotes and other such important details.

subdirectory — A directory within a directory. These subdirectories are useful for organizing programs and data on a hard disk. One might think of subdirectories in terms of a file cabinet. The root directory for the disk drive corresponds to a multidrawer file cabinet. Each subdirectory would be a file drawer devoted to a certain kind of information like a word-processing program, lectures, research notes, and a book manuscript. In a Macintosh environment, folders are roughly equivalent to subdirectories.

submenu — A menu of options that appears after already having made a choice in a menu.

super computers — The most powerful computers currently available. These machines are used for the most demanding applications, such as weather calculations and for computing tasks such as projections for space satellites. Because most individual campuses do not have the resources to support such a machine, a super computer network has been developed for academic researchers. Those with the need to use such a machine can apply for access to one through their campus computer.

super drive — Disk drive in some Macintosh models capable of reading disks formatted for either the Macintosh System or DOS.

surge protector — Device that resides between the electrical outlet and the computer that protects the computer from any unexpected increase in voltage. These spikes can damage the computer's components.

synchronous communication — The transmission of data using parallel circuits. Because synchronous communication is much faster than asynchronous communication, it is used within the computer. The longer the distance a synchronous communication travels, the more susceptible it is to interference from its own circuits. Therefore, most communications that have to travel more than a few yards use asynchronous methods.

Sysop — *System operator.* This is the person who manages a bulletin board system or related on-line system. This is the person to contact if the user experiences difficulties with the BBS.

System — The Macintosh's operating system. Part of the System is stored on the computer's ROM; the rest resides in the system folder. The newest version, System 7 was released in 1991, with many enhancements over previous versions.

system disk — Floppy or hard disk that contains the operating system software that a computer has to have to run. Also called a boot disk or, on IBM PC-compatible computers, a DOS disk.

System Folder — Macintosh folder in which operating System files are stored. Included in this folder are the Finder's software fonts that appear in applications' fonts menus, Desk Accessories that appear in the Apple menu, auxiliary files used by the Chooser and control panel Desk Accessories, any updates to ROM programs, and the contents of the Scrapbook.

T

telecommunications — Communications transmitted over telephone lines. These include both voice and data communications.

terabyte — 2^{40} bytes. Measure of storage capacity. As memory and storage devices begin to be measure in terabytes (1,099,511,627,776 bytes or characters), it is possible to envision full-text databases of whole libraries. One terabyte could store the text of 1,200,000 300-page books.

terminal — A device, usually with a keyboard and screen, that communicates with multiuser computer system. Terminals really have only one use — to communicate with the computer to which it is connected. Communications software programs let a microcomputer work as one of these terminals when communicating with a host computer.

thermal printer — Printer that uses heat to print a character on specially treated paper.

timed backup — Also called automatic backup. Certain applications packages provide the option for a file that is currently used to be automatically saved at fixed intervals. This serves as a precaution against accidental damage to a file. To anyone who has lost several hours of writing and revising due to a power outage or some other disaster, these timed backups make a great deal of sense.

token-ring network — A local area network that uses token passing in a ring topology. Information transmitted on the network is preceded by a token that identifies the network node to which the information is being sent. The token is continually passed among the nodes, which are joined by cables that form a circle, but is accepted only by the correct node.

touch-sensitive display — Display that also serves as an input device. The pressure-sensitive panel in the front of the screen lets users select options by simply touching the screen.

track — A concentric circle created on a disk during formatting that defines areas where data can be stored. Each track is further divided into sectors.

trackball — Input device designed as a substitute for the mouse. A ball is partially embedded in the keyboard or a case. As the ball is rotated, the on-screen pointer moves.

translate — Convert a data file from one format to another format.

TSR — *Terminate-and-stay-resident*. A program that remains in the computer's memory for easy access once it is loaded. Usually one keystroke will activate the program again.

twisted-pair cable — Connecting cable used in telephone systems and in some local area networks. The name comes from the two insulated wires that are wrapped around each other. Although twister pair LANs are usually slower than networks based on coaxial cables, they have the distinct advantage of being cheaper.

U

UART — *Universal Asynchronous Receiver/Transmitter*. An integrated circuit used by a computer to transform the data the computer processes in a parallel fashion internally to the serial form used by other devices.

undelete utility — A utility program that undeletes a file that has been deleted. When a file is deleted, the data actually remains on the disk's surface. Its entry is just removed from the file allocation table, which means that area of the disk can be reused by another file. Undelete utilities simply restore the file to the file allocation table. This can only be done if no other file has been written over any part of the previous file. Therefore, if a file is accidentally deleted, do not store any information to the disk until it has been restored.

Unix — Operating system initially developed by Bell Labs that runs on a wide range of computers from PCs to mainframes. Several forms of Unix exist, in part because the antitrust regulations governing AT&T prohibited Bell Labs from marketing it, and it was made available free of charge to colleges and universities in the mid-1970s. However, a Unix standard is now emerging, and it has become the operating system of choice for workstations and other systems. The NeXT computer uses Unix under its own shell, NeXTStep.

upgrade — A new release of a previously existing piece of software.

upload — Transferring files from one computer to another, usually from the remote computer to the host computer. Most communications software have the facilities for accomplishing this transfer.

upward compatibility — Software and hardware that work as well on newer computers as they did with the earlier computer.

user-friendly — A term used to describe software or hardware that is easy to use.

user groups — A group of individuals who join together to share tips and problems about particular kinds of computers or software applications. User groups provide excellent opportunities to learn more about a computer or a piece of software. Often these user groups operate a bulletin board free of charge that can be very helpful for solving problems and getting valuable tips.

user interface — Features of a computer or piece of software that shape the way the user interacts with it.

utilities — Software programs that make a computer more useful to the person using it. These programs accomplish a variety of tasks from recovering lost data to turning off the NumLock key automatically.

V

vaccine — A utility program that detects the presence of a virus in the system and attempts to remove it.

vaporware — A piece of software that has yet to be perfected or marketed.

VDT — *Video Display Terminal*. Synonymous with monitor, display, VDU (video display unit).

VGA — *Video Graphics Array*. Bit-mapped graphics display standard that allows analog monitors to display as many as 256 colors at once with a resolution of 640 by 480 pixels. The Super VGA standard allows 256 colors to be displayed in resolutions as high as 1024 by 768 pixels.

videodisk — Optical disk used to store picture and sound. Most current videodisks can store some 50,000 still frames, or two hours of television pictures.

video RAM — Memory necessary for video adapters to display the high-resolution, multicolor images they are able to produce.

virtual memory — The use of secondary storage devices (such as a hard disk) to extend the available RAM. This technique is commonly used by applications such as word processors so documents or other files need not be limited by RAM size.

virus — A hidden program especially designed to cause unexpected results to the computer's operations. Some of these viruses can be relatively harmless; others can destroy programs or the entire contents of a hard disk. A computer usually catches a virus through shared software; the easiest way to avoid viruses is to use only legal copies of software and avoid downloading software from unknown bulletin board systems. Utility programs are available that test computers for the presence of viruses and then isolate and cure any that are found.

voice entry — Method of entering information into a computer. A person speaks into a receiver connected to a special device that translates the voice patterns into digital representations that the computer can use.

voice mail — Communications system in which telephone messages are stored in digital form on a computer network.

voice recognition systems — Hardware and software systems designed to "hear" and interpret information presented verbally, using pattern recognition techniques. These systems are still limited in what they can accomplish, but they raise interesting possibilities for future uses.

W

wait state — A processing cycle during which nothing happens. These are used to allow slower system components to catch up with faster ones. Computers advertised as having zero wait states use other techniques to let this happen.

wide area network (WAN) — Computer network using high-speed, long-distance communications networks or satellites. These networks stretch over far greater distances than the local area networks, which usually exist in a limited geographic space.

widow — Text editing term used to describe the appearance of the last line of a paragraph on a separate page.

wild card — A symbol that represents a variety of things. Like a wild card in poker, a computer wild card can be used for any other symbol. Common wild-card characters are the asterisk and question mark. A wild-card search for COMPUT* would find COMPUTER, COMPUTERS, COMPUTING, COMPUTATIONAL, and all other words that begin with the letters COMPUT.

windowing environment — A user interface for applications programs that has features common to a graphical user interface. This windowing environment has become an important aspect of most software use and development for IBM PC-compatible machines.

word-processing program — Most historians who use microcomputers do so for word-processing purposes. These applications were designed to make the writing, editing, formatting, and printing of documents easier. Each new release of these word-processing programs adds new features that may or may not be relevant to the kinds of text processing an individual needs.

workstation — High-performance personal computer. These computers are usually equipped with fast processors, high-resolution screens, and large amounts of memory. More expensive than most microcomputers, these machines usually use Unix as an operating system.

WORM — *Write Once, Read Many.* Description for CD-ROMs that refers to the ability to write to the surface of the CD only once, although it can be read many times.

WYSIWYG — *"What You See Is What You Get."* Term usually applied to word processors that let you see on the screen what you will get on the printer. Computers and programs that support the graphical user interface are the most successful at meeting this standard.

X–Z

Xenix — System V-based Unix operating system developed by Microsoft.

XMODEM — File transfer protocol for asynchronous communications.

zap — Erase or delete, depending on the application.

zero-slot LAN — Local area network that uses the serial port or SCSI already on the computer instead of requiring the use of a board in one of the expansion slots.

zoom — To enlarge a window so it fills the whole screen. In some pieces of software, zooming out means to display the whole page or image on the screen while zooming in means to expand a small portion so it fills the screen.

The following sources were particularly useful in compiling this glossary:

Covington, Michael, and Douglas Downing. *Dictionary of Computer Terms, 2nd edition.* New York: Barron's, 1988.

Heid, Jim, and Peter Norton. *Inside the Apple Macintosh.* New York: Simon and Schuster, 1989.

PC Novice magazine.

Pfaffenberger, Bryan. *Que's Computer User's Dictionary.* Carmel, IN: Que Corporation, 1990.

Appendix B: RESOURCE GUIDE

How to Use This Resource Guide

These resources were selected to help the reader sift through the massive literature available on computing. This resource guide is directed toward topics discussed in the text, particularly those terms set in the Helvetica type font.

Software Mentioned in the Pamphlet or Recommended by Contributors

The inclusion of a piece of software in this list is not meant as a product endorsement. In the course of researching this book, I consulted colleagues who use computers in their research or teaching; hence the mention of partricular software programs and their functions. For those interested in a complete list of software available, along with reviews of that software, there are several sources to consult. For those looking for very generalized comparisons, a good source is *Software Digest* or *Data Pro*, which might be called the *Consumer Reports* for software.

Computer magazines also provide regular reviews of software and hardware. *Computerworld, Infoworld,* and *Byte* cover a variety of machine types in their surveys and reviews. Good choices for the IBM PC-compatible world include *PC Magazine, PC Novice, PC World,* and *PC Week.* Macintosh users might consult *Mac Week, MacWorld,* or *MacUser.* All of these magazines are generally available, so publication information is not included below. These are also indexed on both CD-ROM and on Dialog. Anyone with access to those indexes will be able to locate these reviews quite quickly.

Buyers' guides for software (these exist for both the Macintosh and the PC) list literally hundreds of pieces of software by category. Although they do not provide detailed information, they certainly give users interested in a type of software some notion of what possibilities are available to them. These guides are published quarterly and are available at many bookstores.

Historians will also find the software reviews in the following journals to be quite useful: *Social Science Computer Review, Computers and the Humanities, History Microcomputer Review, Bits and Bytes Review,* and *History and Computing.* Because these journals are aimed at historians, social scientists, or humanists, they often look at software applications that are relevant to historians.

The best sources of information on software and hardware are often colleagues. There are two reasons for this. The first is that a colleague often knows the kind of application you will use and can respond more directly to your particular needs. The second reason is that there is a critical mass of other users who can provide assistance if you need it. You might remain convinced that Ami Pro is the best word-processing program, but if everyone on your campus is using Word, you might find that simple problems using the former become much bigger if the only place you can get advice is by calling the manufacturer.

Weigh any advice, however, with some research of your own. Almost everyone tends to like the software and hardware she or he uses. What is a wonderful setup for one person is not necessarily a wonderful setup for another for reasons ranging from typing speed to research preferences to previous computer experience.

Communications

Communications software often comes packaged with a *modem* at no cost or is distributed by colleges and universities for use with their particular network. Electronic bulletin boards often contain quite workable public domain telecommunications packages as well. Those listed below are among the best known of the commercial packages.

ProComm	DataStorm Technologies, Inc., PO Box 1471, Columbia, MO 65205 (PC)
Smartcom II	Hayes Microcomputer Products, Inc. PO Box 105203 Atlanta, GA 30348 (Mac and PC)
VersaTerm	Synergy Software 2457 Perkiomen Ave. Reading, PA 19606 (PC and Mac)

Databases

Databases come in a variety of forms. Therefore, the choice of a database depends on what task is expected of it. Fixed-field databases are appropriate for storing data that have common forms such as census records, economic data, grades, and any number of other types of information. Free-field databases are more useful for notes and data that have no preordained structures. Some individuals take advantage of the database options built into spreadsheet programs, text managers, hypertext, and personal information management (PIM) programs and use them instead of databases. Increasingly, the various types of database management systems are beginning to resemble each other. To insure a good fit between software and application, the user should decide what the software is needed for before buying it, rather than buying the software and then trying to fit the data into something less than appropriate.

Fixed-Field Databases

dBASE dBASE IV and previous versions	Ashton Tate 20101 Hamilton Ave. Torrance, CA 90502 (Mac and PC)
Double Helix	Odesta Corp. 4084 Commercial Ave. Northbrook, IL 60062 (Mac and Vax)
Filevision IV	TSP Software 4790 Irvine Blvd., Suite 105–294, Irvine, CA 92720 (Mac)
FoxPlus	Fox Software, Inc. 134 W. South Boundary Perrysburg, OH 43551 (Mac and PC)
Paradox	Borland International, Inc. 1800 Green Hills Rd. Scotts Valley, CA 95066

Free-Field Databases

AskSam	AskSam Systems P.O. Box 1428, 119 S. Washington St. Perry, FL 32347 (PC)
BiblioStax	Pro/Tem Software 994 Loma Verde Ave. Palo Alto, CA 94303 (Mac)
EndNote Plus	Niles & Associates,Inc. 2000 Hearst St. Berkeley, CA 94709 (Mac)

InMagic	Inmagic Corp.
	2067 Massachusetts Ave.
	Cambridge, MA 02140 (PC)

Notebook II — Pro/Tem Software
994 Loma Verde Ave.
Palo Alto, CA 94303

(or as Notebook II Plus with AHA discount)
Oberon Resources
147 East Oakland Ave.
Columbus, OH 43201 (PC)

Pro-Cite — Personal Bibliographic Software, Inc.
P.O. Box 4250
Ann Arbor, MI 48106 (Mac and PC)

Squarenote — UnionSquareware
27 St. Mary's Court
Brookline, MA 02146 (PC)

Hypermedia, Hypertext

More new hypermedia and hypertext programs are appearing than any other kind of software. No clear standards have emerged as yet and the variety of programs and add-ons is growing almost daily. The two best-known of this type of software are:

Guide — Owl International, Inc.
2800 156th Ave. SE
Bellevue, WA 98007 (PC and Mac)

HyperCard — Claris Corp.
5201 Patrick Henry Dr.,
PO Box 58168
Santa Clara, CA 95052 (Mac)

Mapping

Mapping software ranges from inexpensive packages available from academic software repositories to very expensive systems designed for scientific and market analysis. Map outlines are becoming more generally available as well, especially on CD-ROM. The piece of mapping software most widely used by contributors to this pamphlet was:

Atlas MapMaker	Strategic Mapping, Inc.
Atlas GIS	4030 Moorpark Ave., Suite 250,
	San Jose, CA 93021
	408-985-7400 (PC and Mac)

Spreadsheets

Different spreadsheet programs are very much variations on the same basic program. They all contain the basic worksheet of rows and columns, simple graphic presentations, and some database functions.

Lotus 1-2-3	Lotus Development Corporation
	55 Cambridge Parkway
	Cambridge, MA 02412 (PC)
Microsoft Excel	Microsoft Corporation,
	16011 N. E. 36th Way, P. O. Box 97017
	Redmond, WA 98073 (Mac and PC)
Quattro Pro	Borland International, Inc.
	1800 Green Hills Rd.
	Scotts Valley, CA 95066 (PC)
Wingz	Informix Software, Inc.
	4100 Bohannon Dr.
	Menlo Park, CA 94025 (Mac)

Statistical Analysis

The number of statistical analysis packages available on microcomputers is quite impressive. As is apparent in the list below, most large mainframe statistics packages have been migrated downward to run on microcomputers. Many of them have only recently begun to take advantage of the particular strengths of the microcomputer environment, including graphical capabilities and a more user-friendly environment. There are specialized statistical packages for particular types of analysis and several smaller packages developed primarily for teaching. Reviews of these statistical packages that evaluate both their statistical and computer strengths appear in the journals of the disciplines most likely to use them.

Datadesk	Odesta Corporation 4084 Commercial Northbrook, IL 60062 (Mac)
SAS	SAS Institute, Inc. SAS Circle, Box 8000 Cary, NC 27512 (PC)
SPSS	SPSS, Inc. 444 N. Michigan Ave. Chicago, IL 60610 (Mac, PC, other mini and mainframe computers)
Systat	Systat, Inc. 1800 Sherman Ave. Evanston, IL 60201 (PC, Mac, other mini and mainframe computers)

Text Retrieval

These programs allow the user to search the contents of groups of files or the entire hard drive for particular words, phrases, or combinations of the two. They are very useful for locating information and managing notes.

Gofer	Microlytics, Inc. 2 Tobey Village Office Park Pittsford, NY 14534 (Mac)
Magellan	Lotus Development Corporation 55 Cambridge Parkway Cambridge, MA 02412 (PC)
Marco Polo	Mainstay 5311-B Derry Ave. Agoura Hills, CA 91301 (Mac)

Utilities

There are utility programs designed to accomplish any task on a computer, from capturing a printing task to a file to compacting files to turning off the NumLock key. Many of these that are devoted to a single task are public domain or shareware. There are also several utility programs that any computer user should have or might find very useful. These are listed here under Hard Disk Utilities.

Antivirus Programs

Viruses have become a very serious problem for computer users, especially those who share software or who download programs and information from bulletin boards. These viruses are hidden programs that can cause serious damage to files stored on disks. Antivirus programs isolate these viruses and try to prevent or repair any damage. They are not failsafe, however, because people who create viruses devote much time to trying to devise new viruses that are harder to detect. The best way to protect against viruses is to use only legal software.

AntiToxin	Mainstay 5311-B Derry Ave. Agoura Hills, CA 91301 (Mac)
Norton Anti-Virus (for PC) Symantec Anti-Virus (for Mac)	Symantec Corp. 10201 Torre Ave. Cupertino, CA 95014 (PC and Mac)
Virex	Microcom, Inc. Utilities Product Group P.O. Box 51489 Durham, NC 27717 (Mac)

File Conversion

These programs translate files stored in the format of one program into the format of another program. These are especially useful when it is necessary to move documents between one word-processing package and another. They are also useful when moving information between the PC and the Macintosh environment.

Software Bridge	Systems Compatibility Corp. 401 N. Wabash, Suite 600 Chicago, IL 60611 (Mac and PC)
Word for Word	Mastersoft, Inc. 6991 Camelback Rd. Scottsdale, AZ (PC and Mac)

File Transfer

These programs facilitate the transfer of files from one computer to another. They generally involve the use of a cable connecting two machines that permit direct transfers rather than using disks. The utilities that link the Mac and the PC translate the files to the correct format of the receiving machine as well.

Brooklyn Bridge	Fifth Generation Systems, Inc. 10049 N. Reigh Rd. Baton Rouge, LA 70809 (PC)
Lap Link	Traveling Software, Inc. 18702 N. Creek Pkwy. Bothell, WA 98011 (Mac and PC)
MacLinkPlus	Dataviz, Inc. 35 Corporate Dr. Trumbull, CT 06611 (Mac and PC)

Hard Disk Utilities

These utilities contain a number of different programs that help manage and protect the contents of hard disks. The most immediately valuable modules are those that unerase and rebuild files. They also contain modules that optimize disk performance, locate information on the disk, and do other such tasks. Every computer user should probably own one of the many packages that provide these functions.

Norton Utilities Symantec Utilities	Symantec Corp. 10201 Torre Ave. Cupertino, CA 95014
Mac Tools Deluxe PC Tools Deluxe	Central Point Software, Inc. 15220 NW Greenbrier Pkwy, #200 Beaverton, OR 97006

Multitasking

DesqView	Quarterdeck Office Systems 150 Pico Blvd. Santa Monica, CA 90405 (PC)

Microsoft Windows	Microsoft Corporation
	16011 N. E. 36th Way
	P. O. Box 97017
	Redmond, WA 98073
	(This provides much more than just multitasking—it provides a graphical user interface for the PC as well.)

Word Processing

No piece of software is as much a matter of personal preference to a scholar as a word-processing package. The look and feel of the software is critical to how one writes. Before buying a piece of software, decide what you want it to do (i.e., does it easily let you transform footnotes to endnotes, does it allow outlining, how effective is its indexing capability, does it allow simple desktop publishing, can your publisher take files directly from your program, does it work with the laser printers on campus). Then see if you can try it out before buying it. A very fast typist, for example, might resent having to use a mouse to accomplish simple tasks because it removes the hands from the keyboard. Another who does much cutting and pasting might find the mouse the best device for enhancing writing. Most word processors keep up with the advances of other word processors, so the most popular programs maintain a kind of rough equivalency over time.

Ami Pro	Lotus Development Corporation
	55 Cambridge Parkway
	Cambridge, MA 02412 (PC??)
MacWrite	Claris Corp.
	5201 Patrick Henry Dr., P. O. Box 58168
	Santa Clara, CA 95052 (Mac?)
Microsoft Word	Microsoft Corp.
	16011 N. E. 36th Way, P.O. Box 97017
	Redmond, WA 98073
	(PC and Mac, also for Windows)
Nota Bene	Dragonfly Software
N.B. Ibid	285 W. Broadway, #500
	New York, NY 10013
	(PC, includes text-oriented database; endorsed by the MLA)

WordPerfect	WordPerfect Corp. 1555 N. Technology Way Orem, UT 84057 (PC and Mac)
WriteNow	T/Maker Co. 1390 Villa St. Mountain View, CA 94041 (Mac)
Xywrite	Xyquest 44 Manning Rd. Billerica, MA 01821 (PC)

A variety of add-on software packages have emerged that help with the writing process. Software examples of various types of these include the following:

Correctamente	Medina Software, Inc. P.O. Box 52197 Longwood, FL 32752 (Spanish spelling checker for Mac)
Grammatik	Reference Software International 330 Townsend, Suite 123 San Francisco, CA 94107 (expert system grammar and style checker for word-processing documents — PC and Mac)
NLCindex	Newberry Library 60 W. Walton Chicago, IL 60610 (indexing program to create scholarly indexes — PC)

Desktop Publishing

Desktop-publishing packages take word processing one step further. They give the person using them almost complete control over the layout of the page, including both images and text. As the software becomes more sophisticated, it becomes possible to use it to create documents that look almost indistinguishable from typeset documents. In fact, some of these packages can even drive typesetting machines. Among the best known of these are the following:

PageMaker	Aldus Corp. 411 First Ave S., Ste. 200 Seattle, WA 98104 (PC and Mac)

| Ventura Desktop Publisher | Ventura Software, Inc.
15175 Innovation Dr.
San Diego, CA 92128
(PC and Mac) |
| Quark Express | Quark, Inc.
300 S. Jackson St. Suite 100
Denver, CO 80209
(Mac) |

Graphics

It is virtually impossible to do justice to microcomputer graphics software in a brief discussion like this. Many applications like spreadsheets and statistics software contain powerful graphics modules within them. Some, like Harvard Graphics and Microsoft Chart, were initially designed to make the creation of charts and graphs easier. Drawing programs like MacDraw, Superpaint, Draw It Again Sam, and PC Paintbrush let their users create their own graphics with a mouse and special-effects tools incorporated into the software. Still others like Freelance Plus and Adobe Illustrator combine the best of both approaches to customize graphics and present them in the most striking possible format. Packages like ClipArt are replete with hundreds of graphics images that can be incorporated into any of these other applications. Finally, CADD (computer-aided drafting and design) programs combine precise graphics with a number of programming and presentation capabilities to let architects, designers, and others create workable models with a computer.

Appendix C: SELECTED BIBLIOGRAPHY

General Useful Overviews to Computers for Those in the Humanities and Social Sciences

Bolter, J. David. *Turing's Man.* Chapel Hill, NC: University of North Carolina Press, 1984.

Brecher, Deborah L. *The Women's Computer Literacy Handbook.* New York: Signet, 1985.

Daedalus 117 (Winter 1988); special issue on artificial intelligence.

Garson, G. David. *Academic Microcomputing: A Resource Guide.* Newbury Park, CA: Sage Publications, Inc.,1986.

Helgerson, L. W. "CD-ROM and Scholarly Research in the Humanities." *Computers and the Humanities* 22 (1988): 111–16.

Hockey, Susan. *A Guide to Computer Applications in the Humanities.* Baltimore, MD: Johns Hopkins, 1980.

Kren, George M., and George Christakes. *Scholars and Personal Computers: Microcomputing in the Humanities and Social Sciences.* New York: Human Sciences Press, 1988.

Lyon, David A. "Promises, Promises." *Lingua franca* 1 (April 1991): 41–42.

Schrodt, Philip A. *Microcomputer Methods for Social Scientists.* Beverly Hills, CA: Sage Publications, 1984.

History

Burton, Vernon, and Terence Finnegan. "Supercomputing and the U.S. Manuscript Census." *Social Science Computer Review* 9 (Spring 1991): 1–12.

Dendieu, J. et al. "Le trésor général des langues et parlers français de l'Institut national de la langue française." *Computers and the Humanities* 22 (1988):67–75.

Denley, Peter, and Deian Hopkin, eds. *History and Computing.* Manchester, U.K.: Manchester University Press, 1987.

————— , with Stefan Fogelvik, and Charles Harvey. *History and Computing II.* Manchester, U.K.: Manchester University Press,1989.

Falk, Joyce Duncan. "Databases for Historical Research: Overview and Implications." *American History: A Bibliographic Review* 4 (1988): 1–13.

Gaffield, Chad. "Machines and Minds: Historians and the Emerging Collaboration." *Histoire sociale/Social History* 21 (November 1988): 312–17.

Gallacher, D. A., and E. D. Treleven. "Developing an Online Database and Printed Directory and Subject Guide to Oral History Collections." *Oral History Review* 16 (Spring 1988): 33–68.

Harvey, Louis-George, and Mark Olson. "Computers and Intellectual History: Lexical Statistics and the Analysis of Political Discourse." *Journal of Interdisciplinary History* 18 (1988): 449–64.

Jensen, Richard. "The Microcomputer Revolution for Historians." *Journal of Interdisciplinary History* 14 (1983): 91–111. Provides an interesting comparison of how computer usage has and has not changed in eight years.

Locicero, Scott. "What on Earth Would a Historian Do with a Microcomputer?" *Proceedings of the Annual Meeting of the Western Society for French History* 12 (1984): 269–77.

Manning, Patrick, and William S. Griffiths. "Divining the Unprovable: Simulating the Demography of African Slavery." *Journal of Interdisciplinary History* 19 (Autumn 1988): 177–201. A simulation model that applies both demographic principles and historical data to the study of African populations influenced by slavery and the slave trade.

Mawdsley, Evan, Nicholas Morgan, Lesley Richmond, and Richard Trainor, eds. *History and Computing III: Historians, Computers and Data* (Manchester, U.K. and New York: Manchester University Press, 1990).

Middleton, Roger, and Peter Wardley. "Information Technology in Economic and Social History." *Economic History Review* 43 (November 1990): 667.

Olsen, Mark. "The Language of Enlightened Politics: The Société de 1789 in the French Revolution." *Computers and the Humanities* 23 (1989): 357–64.

Slatta, Richard. "Historians and Microcomputing, 1989." *Social Science Computer Review* 7 (Winter 1989): 446–58

Spaeth, Donald A, comp. *A Guide to Software for Historians.* Glasgow, U.K.: University of Glasgow, Computers in Teaching Initiative Centre for History, 1991.

Weissman, Ronald F. E. "Strategic Directions in Computing and the Historian's Craft." *American History: A Bibliographic Review* 4 (1988): 23–26.

Teaching with Computers — General

Adams, Anthony, and Esnor Jones. *Teaching Humanities in the Microelectronic Age.*. New York: Open University Press, 1983.

Adams, Dennis M., and Mary E. Hamm. *Media and Literacy: Learning in an Electronic Age: Issues, Ideas and Teaching Strategies.* Springfield, IL: C. C. Thomas, 1989.

Balestri, Diane Pelkus et al. *Ivory Towers, Silicon Basements: Learner-Centered Computing in Postsecondary Education.* McKinney, TX: Academic Computing Publications, 1988.

Barker, Philip, ed. *Multimedia Computer Assisted Learning.* East Brunswick, NJ: Nickels Publishing, 1981.

Graves, William H., ed. *Computing Across the Curriculum: Academic Perspectives.* McKinney, TX: Academic Computing Publications, Inc., 1989.

Ide, Nancy M. "Computers and the Humanities Courses: Philosophical Bases and Approach." *Computers and the Humanities* 21 (1987): 209–15.

National Task Force on Educational Technology. "Transforming American Education: Reducing the Risk to the Nation" (Report to the Secretary of Education). *T.H.E. Journal* 14 (1986): 58–67.

Seiden, Peggy, ed. *Directory of Software Applications in Higher Education.* Princeton, NJ: Peterson's Guides, 1987.

Teaching with Computers — History

Burton, Orville Vernon, and Terence Finnegan. "New Tools for Historical Methods." *History Microcomputer Review* 5 (Spring 1989): 13–18.

Crozier, William, and Chad Gaffield. "The Lower Manhattan Project." *Historical Methods* 23 (Spring 1990): 72.

Fitch, Nancy. "The Crisis in History: Its Pedagogical Implications." *Historical Methods* 21 (Summer 1988): 104–11.

Gross, Robert A. "The Machine-Readable Transcendentalists: Cultural History on the Computer." *American Quarterly* 41 (September 1989): 502–21.

Gutmann, Myron P. "Teaching Historical Research Skills to Undergraduates: Thoughts on Microcomputers and the Classroom." *Historical Methods* 21 (Summer 1988): 112–20.

Lougee, Carolyn Chappell. "'The Would-Be Gentleman': A Historical Simulation of the France of Louis XIV." *History Microcomputer Review* 4 (Spring 1988): 7–14.

_____ , and Michael P. Carter. "The Would-Be Gentleman: A Historical Simulation of the France of Louis XIV." In William H. Graves, ed. *Computing Across the Curriculum: Academic Perspectives.* McKinney, TX: Academic Computing Publications, 1989.

McClymer, John F. "Using Database Software in Undergraduate Survey Courses." *Teaching History* 12 (Fall 1987): 10–17.

Miller, David W. "The Great American History Machine." *Academic Computing* 3 (October 1988): 28–29, 43–45.

_____ , and John Modell. "Teaching United States History with the Great American History Machine." *Historical Methods* 21 (Summer 1988): 121–34.

Pycior, Stanley W. "The Future of Teaching the Past: Computer-Assisted Instruction in History." *Computers and the Humanities* 18 (1984): 205–14.

Reiff, Janice L. "Using History to Teach Microcomputers." *Historical Methods* 21 (Summer 1988): 135–39.

Schick, James B. M. *Teaching History With a Computer: A Complete Guide.* Chicago: Lyceum Books, Inc., 1990. This volume provides an excellent summary of a wide variety of computer applications used in history classrooms. It is highly recommended for persons interested in learning about the current state of the microcomputer in the teaching of history.

Semoche, John. "Computer Simulations, the Teaching of History, and the Goals of a Liberal Education." *Academic Computing* 2 (September 1987): 20–23, 46–50.

_____ . "Making History Come Alive: Designing and Using Computer Simulations in U.S. History Survey Courses." *History Microcomputer Review* 5 (Spring 1989): 5–12.

van Hartesveldt, Fred R. "Using Computers in Lower Division History Courses." *Teaching History* 10 (Spring 1985): 27–32.

Xidis, Kathleen. "Students, Microcomputers and Software: A New Approach in History Courses." *History Microcomputer Review* 4 (Fall 1988): 15–20.

Hypertext, Hypermedia

Berrett, E., ed. *The Society of Text: Hypertext and Hypermedia, and the Social Construction of Information.* Cambridge, MA: MIT Press, 1989.

Chignell, Mark H., and Richard M. Lacy. "Project Jefferson: Integrating Research and Instruction." *Academic Computing* 3 (October 1988): 12–17, 40–45.

Crane, Gregory. "The Perseus Project: A Hypermedia Database About Classical Greece." *Syllabus* 5 (April 1989) 9.

—————. "Challenging the Individual: the Tradition of Hypermedia Databases." *Academic Computing* 4 (January 1990): 22–23, 31–32, 34–38.

Friedlander, Larry. "The Shakespeare Project: Experiments in Multimedia Education." *Academic Computing* 2 (May/June 1988): 26–29+.

Havholm, Peter L., and Larry L. Stewart. *Using OWL International Inc.'s GUIDE to Teach Critical Thinking*. MSS, College of Wooster (Ohio).

Landow, George P. "Hypertext in Literary Education, Criticism and Scholarship." *Computers and the Humanities* 23 (1989): 173–98.

Lynch, Patrick. "Finding the Media for Multimedia." *Syllabus* 12 (July–August 1990): 21–22.

Richards, Tyde, Mark H. Chignell, and Richard M. Lacy. "Integrated Hypermedia: Bridging the Missing Links." *Academic Computing* 4 (January 1990): 24–26, 39–44.

Libraries, Archives, and Museums

Arms, Caroline, ed. *Campus Strategies for Libraries and Electronic Information*. Bedford, MA: Digital Press, 1989.

Crawford, David. "Meeting Scholarly Information Needs in an Automated Environment: A Humanist's Perspective." *College and Research Libraries* 47 (November 1986): 569–74.

Dollar, Charles M. "The Impact of New Technologies on the National Archives and Federal Government Documentation." *American History: A Bibliographic Review* 4 (1988): 14–22.

Dowler, Lawrence. "Conference on Research Trends and Library Resources." *Harvard Library Bulletin* I (Summer 1990): 5–14.

Falk, Joyce Duncan. "OCLC and RLIN: Research Libraries at the Scholar's Fingertips." *Perspectives* 27 (May–June 1989): 1, 11–13, 17.

Morris, Dilys E. "Electronic Information and Technology: Impact and Potential for Academic Libraries." *College and Research Libraries* 50 (1989): 138–75.

Noble, Richard A. "The NHPRC Database Project." *American Archivist* 51 (1988): 98–105.

Networks and Telecommunications

Heid, Jim. "Getting Started with Networks." *MacWorld* 7 (December 1990): 291–95.

Horner, Vivian M., and Linda G. Roberts. "Electronic Links for Learning." Special issue of the *Annals of the American Academy of Political and Social Science* 514 (March 1991).

LaQuey, Tracy. "Networks for Academics." *Academic Computing* 4 (November 1989): 32–34, 39, 65.

Mabry, Donald. "Electronic Mail and Historians." *Perspectives* 29 (February 1991): 1, 4, 6.

Meng, Brita. "Networking for the Novice." *MacWorld* 7 (December 1990): 202–09.

Slatta, Richard W. "Telecommunications for the Humanities and Social Sciences." *Microcomputers for Information Management* 3 (June 1986): 91–110.

Publishing

Burstyn, Joan N., ed. *Desktop Publishing in the University.* Syracuse, NY: Syracuse University Press, 1991.

Crane, Gregory. "Redefining the Book: Some Preliminary Problems." *Academic Computing* 2 (February 1988): 6–11, 36–41.

Daedalus 111 (Fall 1982). Special issue on print and video culture, especially Anthony Smith, "Information Technology and the Myth of Abundance," 1–16; and Itheil de Sola Pool, "The Culture of Electronic Print," 17–31.

Paulson, William. "Computers, Minds, and Texts: Preliminary Reflections." *New Literary History* 20 (Winter 1989): 291–303.

Provenzo, Eugene F. *Beyond the Guttenberg Galaxy: Microcomputers and the Emergence of a Posttypographic Culture.* New York: Columbia University Teachers College Press, 1986.

Seiber, Lauren H. "The Future of the Scholarly Journal." *Academic Computing* 4 (September 1989).

Software Development

Cartwright, G. Phillip, and Carol A. Cartwright. "Software Development: Considerations for Promotion and Tenure." *Academic Computing* 1 (Spring 1987): 14–17, 64–66.

Garson, G. David. "Software Authorship, Software Usership: A Look at Faculty Software Development from the Bottom Up." *Academic Computing* 2 (October 1987): 20–23, 50–52.

Kozma, Robert B., J. Johnston, and Etta Vinik. "New Media for More Classrooms: The 1989 EDUCOM/NCRIPTAL Higher Education Software Award Winners." *EDUCOM Review* 24 (Fall 1989): 44–49.

—————, and Etta Vinik. "Can Software Publishing Keep Faculty from Perishing?" *Syllabus* 9 (January–February 1990): 10–11.

Turner, Judith Axler. "Student Involvement a Common Theme Among Software-Award Winners." *Chronicle of Higher Education* (September 19, 1990): A22–A23.

Word Processing

Balestri, Diane Pelkus. "Softcopy and Hard: Wordprocessing and Writing Process." *Academic Computing* 2 (February 1988): 14–17, 41–45.

Costanzo, William. *The Electronic Text: Learning to Write, Read and Reason With Computers.* Englewood Cliffs, NJ: Educational Technology Publications, 1989.

Di Pasquale, Mauro G. "Beyond Word Processing—Text Management Programs." *Research in Word Processing Newsletter* 6 (April 1988): 10–15.

Kaplan-Neuer, Anne. "Technology and the Writing Process." *Syllabus* 10 (March–April 1990): 2–4.

—————. "Emerging Technologies and Their Impact on Writing Across the Curriculum." Syllabus 10 (March–April): 5–9.

There is also a BITNET bulletin board that is devoted to teaching writing that will provide useful information to anyone interested.

Miscellaneous Computer Applications

"Communication in Archaeology: A Global View of the Impact of Information Technology." *Science and Archaeology* 32 (1990).

Heise, David R. "Computer Analysis of Cultural Structures." *Social Science Computer Review* 6 (Spring 1988): 18—96.

Kiel, L. Douglas. "Thematic Mapping With Microcomputers: Graphic Display of Social Scientific Data." *Social Science Computer Review* 6 (Spring 1988): 197–209.

Tournier, Maurice. "Le vocabulaire des pétitions ouvrières de 1848: étude des parentages statistiques" in Régin Robin, *Histoire et linguistique* (Paris, 1973), 261–303.

Tufte, Edward. *The Visual Display of Quantitative Information* (Cheshire, CT: Graphics Press, 1983) and *Envisioning Information* (Cheshire, CT: Graphics Press, 1990).

Turner, Gene. "Production of Ethnic Map Patterns in Los Angeles," *Occasional Publications in Geography* 5 (1989), Department of Geography, California State University, Northridge.

Wagner, Richard A. "The Rise of Computing in Anthropology: Hammers and Nails." *Social Science Computer Review* 7 (Winter 1989): 418–29.

White, Douglas R., and Gregory F. Truex. "Anthropology and Computing: The Challenges of the 1990s." *Social Science Computer Review* 6 (Winter 1988): 481–97.

Wood, Michael Ray, and Louis A. Zurcher, Jr. *The Development of a Post-Modern Self: A Computer-Assisted Comparative Analysis of Personal Documents* (New York: Greenwood Press, 1988).

Research Centers and Development Projects

American and French Research on the Treasury of the French Language (ARTFL) — A cooperative project begun in 1981 by the Centre national de la recherche scientifique (CNRS) and the University of Chicago. It contains over 2,000 French literary, historical, philosophical, and scientific works published between the seventeenth and nineteenth centuries. Available on-line through Internet for a subscription fee. Contact the ARTFL Project, Department of Romance Languages and Literatures, University of Chicago, 1050 E. 59th St., Chicago, IL 60637. ARTFL@ARTFL.UCHICAGO.EDU or MARK@GIDE.UCHICAGO.EDU. European scholars can obtain information from: l'Institut national de la langue française, Centre national de la recherche scientifique, 52 Boulevard de Magenta, 75010 Paris, France.

American Memory Collections Project. This Library of Congress project is putting a variety of different kinds of important archival material from the Library of Congress on CD-ROM. Further information is available from Special Projects, Library of Congress, Washington, D.C. 20540.

Centre for Computing in the Humanities, University of Toronto. Toronto, Ontario, M5S 1A1, Canada. Ian Lancashire, Director. This center has assumed an important leadership role in the development of organizations and activities for humanists interested in computer applications.

Center for Scholarly Technology, Doheny Library, University of Southern California, Los Angeles, CA90089. Peter Lyman, Director. The Center is devoted to the study and development of applications for computers and related technologies in academic environments.

The Civil War Hypermedia Project is an undertaking of the Center for Interactive Educational Technology (CIET) at George Mason University, in conjunction with Florentine Films. By December of 1990, the development team at the CIET had formulated a detailed plan for using the incredible archive assembled by producer/director Ken Burns for the PBS series *The Civil War* as a basis for an interactive videodisk to supplement the teaching of American history at the secondary and postsecondary levels. Contact: Dr. Lynn Fontana, CIET, George Mason University, Fairfax, VA 22030-4444. Telephone: (703) 993-3641.

Computers in Teaching Intiative Centre for History with Archaeology & Art History (CTICH) — Developed as part of the U.K.'s Computer Teaching Initiative, CTICH serves as a focal point for computer applications in history and related fields for the United Kingdom. It publishes a newsletter, *Craft*, and other documents relevant to computing and history. More information is available from CTICH, University of Glasgow, 1 University Gardens, Glasgow G12 8QQ, Scotland. E-mail: CTICH@UK.AC.GLASGOW.VME.

Computers in Teaching Initiative Support Service (CTISS) — Developed in May 1986 as part of the United Kingdom's Computer Teaching Initiative to encourage the development of computer-assisted teaching and learning in U.K. universities, to evaluate the educational potential of information technology at U.K. universities, and to promote an enhanced awareness of the potential of information technology among lecturers and students in all disciplines. It publishes a regular summary of activities as *The CTISS File*. For information on projects and CTISS in general, contact CTISS, University of Bath, Bath, Avon BA2 7AY, England. JANET Mail Address: ctiss@swurcc

DISH Project: Design and Implementation of Software in History, History Computing Laboratory, 2 University Gardens, University of Glasgow, Glasgow G12 8QQ, Scotland. DISH@UK.AC.GLASGOW.VME. DISH operates under the auspices of Glasgow's Faculty of Arts and is a joint venture of the Departments of Economic History, Modern History, Scottish History, and the University Archives. It also has close ties to the

University's Computing Service, its Computing Science and Medieval History Departments and its Wellcome Unit for the History of Medicine. The University of Glasgow offers an M.Phil. in History and Computing. For further information contact Dr. R. H. Trainor, DISH Project, 2 University Gardens, University of Glasgow, Glasgow G12 8QQ, Scotland. Telephone: 041-339-8855, ext. 4510. E-mail: DISH@UK.AC.GLASGOW.VME

HiDES (Historical Document Expert System) Project: Dr. R. F. Colson, Department of History, University of Southampton, Highfield, Southampton, Hampshire S09 5NH, England.

IRIS Intermedia. Brown University, Providence, RI 02912. IRIS has taken a leading role in the development of hyper- and intermedia projects for academic applications.

Max-Planck-Institut für Geschichte, Göttingen, Germany. The Historical Workstation project is working on a "historical workstation" composed of three key components—software, databases, and knowledge bases. For information on the project and availability of various pieces of software, databases, and knowledge bases, contact Manfred Thaller, research fellow.

NCRIPTAL (National Center for Research to Improve PostSecondary Teaching and Learning), Suite 2400, School of Education Building, University of Michigan, Ann Arbor, MI 48109–1259. As the donor of prizes for best teaching software, NCRIPTAL knows about almost all the teaching software developed in the United States.

A list of significant computerized projects developed over the past decade with the assistance of the National Endowment for the Humanities is available from Reference Materials: Tools Program, Division of Research Programs, Room 318, National Endowment for the Humanities, 1100 Pennsylvania Ave., NW, Washington, DC 20506. Telephone (202) 786-0358.

Data Repositories

Inter-University Consortium for Social and Political Research (ICPSR), P. O. Box 1248, Ann Arbor, MI 48106.

Public On-Line Library (POLL), Roper Center, University of Connecticut, Storrs, CT 06269.

Software Catalogs, Repositories

Chariot Educational Software Collection, 3659 India St., Suite 100C, San Diego, CA 92103.

Conduit, University of Iowa, Oakdale Campus, Iowa City, IA 52242 (319-335-4100). BITNET: AWCCONPA@UIAMVS

Intellimation Library for the Macintosh. P. O. Box 1922, Santa Barbara, CA 93116.

ISAAC (Information System for Advanced Academic Computing) serves as a clearinghouse for information about the use of IBM-compatible software and hardware as instructional aids in higher education. To apply for a free ID, contact ISAAC3 Access, m/s FC-06, University of Washington, Seattle, Washington 98195. Telephone: (206) 543-5604. BITNET: ISAAC3@UWAEE

National Collegiate Software Clearinghouse. NCSC is an affiliate of the *Social Science Computer Review* and distributes instructional and research software for the humanities and social sciences. Software authors interested in this distribution system are encouraged to contact NCSC at 919-737-3067 or write the director at Duke University Press, 6697 College Station, Durham, NC 27708. A catalog of offerings is available by writing or calling NCSC, Duke University Press, 6697 College Station, Durham, NC 27708. Telephone: (919) 684-6837.

Tools for Learning, Courseware Catalog, IBM Academic Information Systems, 472 Wheeler Farm Rd., Milford, CT 06460.

Wisc-Ware, Academic Computing, University of Wisconsin-Madison, 1210 W. Dayton St., Madison, WI 53706. Telephone: (800) 543-3201. Internet: WISCWARE@MACC.WISC.EDU BITNET: WISCWARE@WISCMACC

Text Repositories

Library of America. CD-ROM, Vol. 1, Electronic Text Corporation, 2500 North University Ave., Provo, UT 84604. Telephone: (801) 226-0616. Authors on DISK 1 (495): Henry David Thoreau, Walt Whitman, Henry James, Jack London, Mark Twain, Ralph Waldo Emerson, Nathaniel Hawthorne, Thomas Jefferson, Herman Melville, Benjamin Franklin. Also available: Constitution Papers: U.S. Constitution, The Petition of Rights, Penn's Plan of Union, Thoughts on Government, The Federal Papers, The Magna Carta, Orders of Connecticut, Albany Plan of Union, Common Sense, The Mayflower Compact, English Bill of Rights, Resolves of First Continental Congress, and Resolution for Independence.

Oxford University Computing Service Text Archive. The archive contains an expanding number of full texts including the works of such authors as Jane Austen, Samuel Beckett, Lord Byron, Willa Cather, Lewis Carroll, Benjamin Disraeli, Bob Dylan, Erasmus, Pattie Hearst, Doris Lessing, and Martin Luther King, Jr. Different texts have different use restrictions. For a complete list contact the Oxford Text Archive, OUCS, 13 Banbury Rd., Oxford OX2 6NN, UK. Internet: ARCHIVE@VAX.OXFORD.AC.UK

Commercial On-line Databases

CompuServe. CompuServe, Inc., 5000 Arlington Centre Blvd., Columbus, OH 43220. General purpose on-line system with services ranging from making airline reservations to bulletin boards that provide advice for computer problems.

Dialog. Dialog Information Services, Inc., 3460 Hillview Ave., Palo Alto, CA 94304. Largest of the bibliographic services available. Special after-hours and educational rates are available.

Journals Containing Useful Information about Computing Directed toward Academic Audiences

Academic Computing. Academic Computing Publications, Inc., 200 W. Virginia, Box 804, McKinney, TX 75069.

Bits and Bytes Review. Bits and Bytes Computer Resources, 623 N. Iowa Ave., Whitefish, MT 59937.

Cause/Effect Magazine. CAUSE, 737 29th St., Boulder, CO 80303.

Chronicle of Higher Education. Chronicle of Higher Education, Inc., 1255 23rd St., N.W., Suite 700, Washington, DC 20037.

Collegiate Microcomputer. Rose-Hulman Institute of Technology, Terre Haute, IN 47803.

Computers and Composition. Michigan Technological University, Houghton, MI 49931.

Computers and the Humanities. Kluwer Academic Publishers Group, 101 Philip Dr., Norwell, MA 02061. Journal of the Association for Computers and the Humanities. For membership information, contact Joseph Rudman, Dept. of English, Carnegie Mellon University, Pittsburgh, PA 15213.

Computers and Philosophy Newsletter. Carnegie Mellon University, CDEC, Building B., Pittsburgh, PA 15213.

Computers in the Schools. Haworth Press, Inc., 12 W. 32nd St., New York, NY 10001.

Education and Computing. Elsevier Science Publishers BV, Postbus 211, 1000 AE, Amsterdam, Netherlands.

Educational Technology. Educational Technology Publications, Inc., 720 Palisade Ave., Englewood Cliffs, NJ 07632.

EDUCOM Review. EDUCOM, 777 Alexander Rd., Box 364, Princeton, NJ 08540.

History and Computing. Oxford University Press, Walton St., Oxford OX2 6DP, England. Journal of the Association for History and Computing. Membership is through national organizations. At present, U.S. members must join the Canadian branch. For information, contact Prof. Michael Gervers, Div. of Humanities, Scarborough Campus, University of Toronto, 1265 Military Trail, Scarborough, Ontario, M1C 1A4 Canada.

History Microcomputer Review. Dept. of History, Pittsburg State University, Pittsburg, KS 66762.

HMS Newsletter. The History and Macintosh Society, 734 Elkus Walk #201, Goleta, CA 93117-4151.

Journal of Computer-Based Instruction. Association for the Development of Computer-Based Instruction Systems, Western Washington University, Miller Hall 409, Bellingham, WA 98225.

Journal of Computing in Higher Education. Paideia Publishers, P. O. Box 343, Ashfield, MA 01330.

Literary and Linguistic Computing. Oxford University Press, Walton St., Oxford OX2 6DP, England. Journal of the Association for Literary and Linguistic Computing.

Machine Mediated Learning. Taylor & Francis New York, 79 Madison Ave., New York, NY 10016.

Scholarly Publishing. University of Toronto Press, 63A St. George St., Toronto, Ontario M5S 1A6, Canada

Social Science Computer Review. Duke University Press, P. O. Box 6697 College Station, Durham, NC 27708. This publication replaces both *Social Science Microcomputer Review* and *Computers and the Social Sciences.*

Syllabus. P. O. Box 2716, Sunnyvale, CA 94087–0716 Telephone: (408) 257-9416. Publication for Macintosh educational users.BITNET: SYLLABUS@APPLELINK@APPLE.COM.

T.H.E. Journal (Technological Horizons in Education). Information Synergy, Inc., Box 17239, Irving, CA 92713.

The Writing Notebook: Creative Word Processing in the Classroom. P. O. Box 79, Mendocino, CA 95460 (707-937-2848)